CAREER SUCCESS:

Right Here, Right Now!™

Online Services

Delmar Online
To access a wide variety of Delmar products
and services on the World Wide Web,
point your browser to:

        http://www.delmar.com
        or email: info@delmar.com

To access information on YAPA,
point your browser to:

        http://www.yapa.com

A service of I$\widehat{T}$P®

CAREER SUCCESS:

Right Here, Right Now!™

Peter M. Hess

President/Founder of YAPA®

YAPA®

YOUNG ADULT
PROFESSIONAL
ASSOCIATES INC

Delmar Publishers

an International Thomson Publishing company I(T)P®

Albany • Bonn • Boston • Cincinnati • Detroit • London • Madrid
Melbourne • Mexico City • New York • Pacific Grove • Paris • San Francisco
Singapore • Tokyo • Toronto • Washington

NOTICE TO THE READER

Cover and text design: Connie McKinley

Delmar Staff

Publisher: Susan Simpfenderfer
Acquisitions Editor: Jeff Burnham
Developmental Editor: Andrea Edwards Myers
Production Manager: Wendy A. Troeger
Marketing Manager: Katherine Hans

For more information, contact:

Delmar Publishers
3 Columbia Circle, Box 15015
Albany, New York 12212-5015

International Thomson Publishing - Europe
Berkshire House
168-173 High Holborn
London, WC1V7AA
England

Thomas Nelson Australia
102 Dodds Street
South Melbourne, 3205
Victoria, Australia

Nelson Canada
1120 Birchmount Road
Scarborough, Ontario
Canada, M1K 5G4

International Thomson Editores
Campos Eliseos 385, Piso 7
Col Polanco
11560 Mexico DF Mexico

International Thomson Publishing GmbH
Königswinterer Strasse 418
53227 Bonn
Germany

International Thomson Publishing Asia
221 Henderson Road
#05-10 Henderson Building
Singapore 0315

International Thomson Publishing - Japan
Hirakawacho Kyowa Building, 3F
2-2-1 Hirakawacho
Chiyoda-ku, Tokyo 102
Japan

1 2 3 4 5 6 7 8 9 10   XXX   04 03 02 01 00 99 98

ISBN 0-7668-1153-0

DEDICATION

This book is dedicated to you, the aspiring professional,
with sincere hopes and wishes
that you achieve all the success
your mind is capable of imagining.

—PETER M. HESS

CONTENTS

Preface—Success Starts Here: Step Right In   xi

Acknowledgments   xvi

Self-Assessment—Before You Get Started   xix

CHAPTER ONE: SUCCESS as a Path of Life 1

Defining Success   2

Discovering Who You Are: Your Values   2

Discovering Who You Are: Your Beliefs   13

Discovering Who You Are: Your Self-belief   18

Your Basis for Success   20

Determining What You Want to Accomplish: Your Dreams   20

Determining What You Want to Accomplish: Your Goals   23

Formulating Your Action Plan   28

Following Your Path to Success   31

How Close Are You to Success?   34

CHAPTER TWO: SUCCESS in the Job Search **41**

At the Crossroads of Success	42
Matching Yourself to a Career	43
Setting a Career Objective	53
Components of a Successful Job Search	55
Conducting a Successful Job Search	56
Making It Happen for You! Nancy Link, Vice President Thomson University, ITP	64
Developing a Personalized Job Search	67
Writing Your Resumé	73
Resumé Requirements	83
Obtaining References and Letters of Recommendation	83
Writing Cover Letters	84
Preparing a Portfolio	86
Completing Employment Applications	87
Launching Your Job Search	87
Attaining and Maintaining a Positive Attitude	87

CHAPTER THREE: SUCCESS Before, During, and After the Interview **93**

Types of Interviews	94
Preparing for the Interview	95
Making It Happen for You! Connie Davis, The Arc of the United States	101
What Interviewers Look For in a Candidate	102
How Interviewers Treat Candidates	103
How to Put Your Best Foot Forward in an Interview	104
Handling Typical and Tough Interview Questions	110

The All-Important Follow-up Letter 116
Second Interviews 120
When You Are Not Selected For a Job 121
When You Are Offered a Job 122
Assessing a Job Offer 124
The Art of Negotiating: Salary, Benefits, Perks 129
Declining a Job Offer 130
Accepting a Job Offer 130

CHAPTER FOUR: SUCCESS Through Networking 133

What Is Networking? 134
Informal Versus Formal Networking 134
The Win/Win Aspects of Networking 136
Making It Happen For You! Michelle Buenau-Ciccone, AT&T 137
Being Open to Opportunities 138
Promoting Yourself 139
Paying Attention 140
Taking Action 143
Getting Involved 152
Volunteering 152
Appreciating Those Who Make Success a Little Easier 157

CHAPTER FIVE: SUCCESS On the Job 165

Obtaining Support For Your Vision 166
Knowing the Requirements of Your Job 167
Cultivating the Right On-the-Job Attitude 167
Assembling a Working Wardrobe 169
Making It Happen For You! Julie Rosenthal,
Banta Integrated Media 170
Basic Communication Skills 172

Listening 172

Speaking 175

Effective Conversations 177

Speaking on the Telephone 178

Writing 180

Managing Your Time 183

Procrastination 183

"I Just Don't Have Enough Time!" 185

Wasting and Misusing Time 188

Managing Your Time 191

Being Organized is Key 191

Time Management Tools 196

Your Planner 196

Strategies for Managing Your Time 201

Meeting the Demands of Others 201

Just Say No 202

Using Bits and Pieces of Time 202

CHAPTER SIX: **SUCCESS** for life 207

How Mentors Assist in Achieving Goals 208

Finding and Working with a Mentor 209

Becoming a Mentor 212

How Life-long Learning Contributes
to Life-long Success 213

Ways to Become a Life-long Learner 214

Building Blocks of Commitment to Success 221

Soaring to Success 221

Self-Assessment—After You've Finished 225

SUCCESS: Interview Notes 227

PREFACE

SUCCESS Starts Here: Step Right In

My career path has taken me on a journey of a thousand miles, and that same journey is ahead of you. Whether you're still in college, just graduated, or in the middle of changing careers, you probably feel too overwhelmed to even think about taking that first step on your journey. I'm here to help you do that, to act as a guide along the way, and to shake your hand when you achieve career success.

What's involved in taking the first step? I've found that most people who attain career success took the time to realize what makes them unique—their personal qualities, skills, interests, beliefs, and values and to understand what they want from a career—for example, working with technology or having the opportunity for job advancement.

They then explored a range of careers and focused on those that seemed to be good matches for them. Next, they narrowed those matches to one or two occupations that were appealing and then they set a career objective.

Think of a career objective as a target. If you have a target to aim for, you're more likely to hit it. If you know what you want to do, you're more likely to find a satisfying job. Without a target, you're likely to take a job at random, which ultimately will leave you feeling dissatisfied, discouraged, and at a dead end.

> ❝A journey of a thousand miles must begin with a single step.❞
>
> LAO-TZU,
> ANCIENT CHINESE
> PHILOSOPHER

After setting a career objective, successful individuals developed a step-by-step plan for achieving their objective and then put their plan into action. Some people found jobs within a week; others job hunted for months before finding the right career opportunity. All of them realized that finding a job was hard work. They also discovered that the feelings of rejection and dejection experienced along the way often tested them even if they were the most motivated of job and career seekers.

I know first hand all the challenges of finding a job and building a career. I was an art major in high school, who loved being creative and enjoyed writing. So when I went to college, I studied public relations, and I also started a concert-promoting business. That combination landed me the opportunity to finish my undergraduate study at Disney University in Florida where I studied corporate management.

Having received my BS in Public Relations and having completed my work for Disney, I was filled with high hopes of getting a high paying job. But to my dismay I was only offered an entry level position, which for the living standards of the Orlando area was not enough income for me to support myself. So I returned to my college town of Utica in upstate New York.

Everybody that I'd known from college had moved on. The one person I did know who was still there managed an insurance company. When he introduced me to some young people at that company, I couldn't believe it. They were making the incomes I had expected I would make, and they were my age—only 24 years old!

My mind set had always been that money is what makes the world go around. My parents taught me that the path to success was to go to a four-year college, earn a degree, get a good job, work 9 to 5, and make good money. Even when I was in college, the professors made it seem as if we were all going to receive great job offers because of our educations. And here I was educated in my chosen field, and the best I could do was get an entry level job offer. Compared to what these twenty-somethings were making selling insurance, that offer was not my idea of a great job.

Making money was important, and I didn't see it happening for me. As soon as I saw my peers making fantastic livings in the insurance business, I completely forgot about all my goals in life—my art, my need for creativity, and my writing. I didn't pay any attention to what I enjoyed doing. I paid attention to the almighty dollar and nothing else.

So I took a job that required me to do things that I disliked most—cold calling on the telephone and going into the homes of retirement-age strangers in the evenings to talk about, well...death, actually. A far cry from the Magic Kingdom. I was basically a shy person, and I disliked doing these things. I also couldn't, and felt guilty trying to, relate to the needs of retirees. But because the money was weighing so heavily on my mind, I pushed, and I worked, and, like those I had met 12 months ago, I, too, was very successful my first year.

I was one of the top salespersons for the year, I went to conventions galore, and then I won a trip to the 1995 US Open in Long Island. As I was sitting on the 9th green, I remember looking around and seeing crowds of young, successful people. And I thought: wouldn't it be great if there was a way for me to meet individuals like this every day? I'd feel comfortable talking to them about insurance because I could relate to their needs. And before I made it back home, I had come up with the idea that I was going to start a young professional networking organization. I came up with the name YAPA®—Young Adult Professional Associates, Inc.—a name everyone could remember!

When I returned home, I talked to a few of the other young people in the insurance company about my idea—starting an organization to not only meet other young people but to create a center of influence for each of us to learn and to grow from one another in our careers—and they thought it was a great idea.

We had our first event—a social mixer at a restaurant—in September 1995, and 250 people showed up. The comments I heard all night were: "I didn't know that this many young professionals lived in our city."

Word about YAPA® spread quickly. Suddenly the wheels started turning, and I was receiving phone calls from all over the United States—talking to other young people, being creative, being asked to speak at events. That's when I realized that I'd been kidding myself about being in the insurance business. Sure I was making good money, but I didn't enjoy the work. It didn't involve any of the things I liked to do or that I felt I was good at. So this big-time, big-bucks approach wasn't giving me the great job I'd hoped for either. I had to find something else to do to earn a living, but I wasn't sure what that was. At least at the time.

The more I talked to people the more I realized that YAPA® had the potential to be more than just an organization to get young professionals together. I started thinking about that potential and that got me researching and planning the possibilities. The element that came up time and time again in my research was education.

When I spoke with employers, they told me that they were frustrated with incredibly intelligent young people coming out of school who knew nothing about time management, how to run a meeting, or how to dress for a career. When I spoke with college students, they told me that they lacked the confidence to go into the interview process and then to enter the professional atmosphere. I knew this to be true because I felt the same way when I finished college.

That's when it clicked. That's when I knew what I could provide to both employers and to young professionals—a single organization offering career success through resources, services, education, networking, and cutting-edge technology. I already had the organization—YAPA®—I just needed to expand my vision from a simple networking system to a multi-faceted career-support organization. And that's when I set YAPA® on its present course.

You can learn a lot from me; we can learn a lot from each other. Not that I'm a card-carrying, know-everything expert, but what I have learned sometimes takes people most of their lives to realize: You may or may not make a high income in your first job out of college. Financial success is incremental and takes a long time. Going after money alone won't make you happy. What will make you happy is knowing who you are, what you want to achieve and using your skills and abilities to get you where you want to go. Your ideas of where you want to go are going to change throughout your life. After all, my first goal was to get into public relations, and that goal changed as I did. What doesn't change is the need to have someone along for the ride to help you sort out the twists and turns of the journey. You'll find that partner for success in YAPA®, and this book is your guidebook along the path.

Within these pages you'll find expert advice on planning your career, beginning your job search, entering an interview with confidence, advancing your career opportunities through networking, and succeeding on the job and throughout your career. You'll find assignments and exercises to help you clarify your thinking about yourself, your job aspirations, and your career goals. You will find stories of successful people, sharing the career secrets they learned on their career journey. This is *the* book you will want to keep and use as a resource after graduation.

Right here, right now, turn the page and take that single step that will lead you on your own journey of a thousand miles—a journey that is your own successful, rewarding career. Are you ready to start succeeding? Great! Let's get started!

ACKNOWLEDGMENTS

FROM THE AUTHOR

A very warm and heartfelt thank you to everyone who not only believed in YAPA®, but were willing to sacrifice in order to turn a dream into a reality.

To my associates at YAPA®—Dave Zumpano, Joe Savage, Kevin Eldred, Bob Sacks, Tim Ahern, and Rob Hilton. Also to my fellow Utica College of Syracuse University alums Ann Marie Teitelbaum, class of 1992 and Rob Wuest, class of 1989. I can't thank you enough for all you have enabled me to do.

And I could never forget the support from Nigar and Michael Hale, Lawson and Sheila Whiting, Bill Cunningham, Tony Dwyer, Thereasa Sheehan, Lawson Whiting, Jr., Trevor Whiting and the folks at Second Bedroom Studios, Kelly Holgate, Jim Peake, John Stackpole, Steve Szmurlo, Jason P. LaManna, Pauline Bartel, Michelle Buenau-Ciccone, the staff at International Thomson Publishing, Banta Integrated Media, and AT&T WorldNet Service for their contributions and support. I thank you all.

Thanks also to Linda McGraw, Director of Student Career Services at LeMoyne College and the LeMoyne College 1998 summer students who helped to contribute to YAPA®'s understanding of what students wanted to learn about career success.

And last, but certainly not least, a special thanks to my Mom and Dad for their encouragement, courage, patience, inspiration, and for being my best friends. You are the reason for my success. Thank you.

The author and Delmar Publishers would also like to thank those individuals who reviewed the manuscript and participated as interviewees. They all offered helpful, creative, and insightful suggestions and feedback, and as a result of their work, the content of this book reflects the professional efforts of all. Their knowledge and wisdom, so freely given, is greatly appreciated.

REVIEWERS

Kristina Belanger
National Institute for Paralegal Arts
    and Sciences
Boca Raton, Florida

John Bradac
Ithaca College
Ithaca, New York

Denise Carr
Beta Tech
N. Charleston, South Carolina

Michelle Buenau-Ciccone
AT&T
Albany, New York

Joann Driggers
Mt. San Antonio College
Walnut, California

Joyce Eyles
Masters Institute
San Jose, California

Mirian Graddick
AT&T
Basking Ridge, New Jersey

Nancy Link
International Thomson Publishing
Albany, New York

Karen McGrath
Educational Consultant
Colorado Springs, Colorado

Linda McGraw
LeMoyne College
Syracuse, New York

Lynn Meyers
Bryant & Stratton
Buffalo, New York

John Re
Forrest College
Anderson, South Carolina

Maris Roze
DeVry Institutes
Oakbrook, Illinois

Linda Schulte
Southern California University for
    Professional Studies
Santa Ana, California

Reta Stanley
Bryant & Stratton
Liverpool, New York

Kathleen Trivelli
Denver Technical College
Colorado Springs, Colorado

Kathleen Woughter
Alfred University
Alfred, New York

INTERVIEWEES

Michelle Buenau-Ciccone
AT&T
Albany, New York

Connie Davis
The Arc of the United States
Arlington, Texas

Nancy Link
International Thomson Publishing
Albany, New York

Julie Rosenthal
Banta Integrated Media
Cambridge, Massachusetts

FROM THE PUBLISHER

Delmar Publishers wishes to acknowledge one person who deserves a very special acknowledgment and thank you—Pauline Bartel. Pauline, on very short notice, with unrealistic schedules, and with a great deal of enthusiasm and dedication, managed to craft and massage the original manuscript into a final product that we can all be proud of by working closely with the author, Delmar Publishers' staff, and the content reviewers. We are all grateful for her efforts, professionalism, and poise under pressure. Thank you, Pauline.

SELF-ASSESSMENT

Read each of the following statements. Then check "yes," or "maybe," or "no" to indicate whether the statement applies to you right now.

1. I can explain my most important values and beliefs to another person.

    ❑ Yes   ❑ Maybe   ❑ No

2. I have a dream for my future.

    ❑ Yes   ❑ Maybe   ❑ No

3. I have action plans for achieving my goals.

    ❑ Yes   ❑ Maybe   ❑ No

4. I can match my skills and interests to one or more suitable occupations by using career resources.

    ❑ Yes   ❑ Maybe   ❑ No

5. I have a good resumé and can write a good cover letter.

    ❑ Yes   ❑ Maybe   ❑ No

6. I am good at preparing for and undergoing job interviews.

    ❑ Yes   ❑ Maybe   ❑ No

7. I am good at understanding the needs of other people.

    ❑ Yes   ❑ Maybe   ❑ No

8. I am an active listener who respects the speaker and understands the speaker's message.

    ❑ Yes   ❑ Maybe   ❑ No

9. I am a good speaker, with good voice qualities and good command of standard English.

    ❑ Yes   ❑ Maybe   ❑ No

10. I use a planner and a "to do" list to organize my time.

    ❑ Yes   ❑ Maybe   ❑ No

11. I can evaluate whether a job fits into my long-term professional goals.

    ❑ Yes   ❑ Maybe   ❑ No

12. I enjoy learning new things.

    ❑ Yes   ❑ Maybe   ❑ No

Review your self-assessment. Check the statements to which you answered "maybe" or "no." These statements show areas of potential growth for you. Pay special attention to the chapters that address these areas as you move through the book. Good luck!

CHAPTER ONE

SUCCESS as a Path of Life

You don't need a crystal ball to predict the successful future that awaits you. By knowing two things—who you are and what you want—you are primed to enjoy a successful life. Then you'll create your successful life by imagining a vision of the future, formulating a plan of action to get there, and enacting your plan with specific steps. This chapter will help you to accomplish those vital tasks.

After completing this chapter, you should understand:

■ the essence of success

■ the values, beliefs, and self-belief that have made you the person you are

■ your deepest dreams and wishes and how they can become the foundation for your goals

■ how to set goals and develop an action plan to achieve those goals

■ how to overcome success barriers

■ how to monitor your progress on the path to success

> *"The best way to predict the future is to create it."*
>
> PETER F. DRUCKER,
> ECONOMIST,
> JOURNALIST AND
> AUTHOR

DEFINING SUCCESS

According to the French novelist Alexandre Dumas, "Nothing succeeds like success." But what exactly is success? Some people believe that wealth or fame are hallmarks of success. For others, though, success is measured not by one's net worth but by one's self-worth.

These individuals feel positive about themselves and feel fulfilled in all areas of their lives. They seize each new day as an opportunity to grow and to develop to their greatest potential. They view success not as transitory stopping points but as a path that winds through life. And they are successful. Their secret?

They know who they are and what they want. They defined success for themselves, created a vision of the future, and constructed a plan of action to get there. They enacted their plan of action by putting one foot in front of the other on their life's path and began their journey of a thousand miles.

Do you know who you are? Do you know what you want to accomplish? The answers to these questions can be found through self-discovery.

DISCOVERING WHO YOU ARE: YOUR VALUES

Research shows that successful people live by a set of values. Values are your core thoughts and feelings about yourself and about life, which lead you to make decisions and to act in a certain way based on those thoughts and feelings. For example, you may identify with the value of honesty. If so, you will tell the truth because you think that lying is wrong. You will feel betrayed when a person you trust lies to you. You will take action to correct a mistake rather than covering up the error or blaming someone else.

These three aspects of values—thoughts, feelings, and actions—are meant to operate harmoniously. But sometimes one or more aspects are in conflict. If someone invites you to an event that you don't want to attend, you might decide to lie and say that you've already made plans to go somewhere else that day. Afterwards you will probably feel uncomfortable because your thought that lying is wrong is at odds with your action of telling a lie. Research shows that people feel the best in circumstances during which the three aspects of their values are in harmony.

You acquired your values during childhood through the influences of your family and friends, your religion and your cultural heritage, and through the influences of school, the media, and modern society. But you may not be consciously aware of the range of values that have formed you as a person.

Awareness of your values increases your understanding of yourself and the level of satisfaction you feel when you make decisions. You can achieve this through values clarification, a process that involves choosing, prizing, and acting upon your values. To get a sense of this process complete the following exercises.

MY VALUES—PART 1

■ *PURPOSE:* To identify your values and to determine what is important to you.

Following is an alphabetical list of values. Review the list then rank the importance of each value to you in ascending order. Place a (1) next to the value that holds the most importance to you, and place a (15) next to the value that holds the least importance to you. Consider your rankings carefully and spend enough time with this exercise so that the rankings accurately reflect your values.

Value	Rank
Ambitious	_____
Autonomy	_____
Cheerfulness	_____
Competence (capability)	_____
Courteousness (being well-mannered)	_____
Forgiveness	_____
Helpfulness (working for the welfare of others)	_____
Honesty	_____
Being Logical	_____
Obedience (being dutiful, respectful)	_____
Open-mindedness	_____
Recognition	_____
Being Responsible	_____
Being Self-controlled (committed)	_____
Wisdom	_____

■ **PURPOSE:** To choose your values and to determine what is most important to you.

Review your list of fifteen value rankings in My Values—Part I and then complete these statements:

1. The value rankings that I am satisfied with are:

_____

_____

_____

_____

2. The value rankings that I am dissatisfied with are:

_____

_____

_____

_____

3. In ranking the values again, the order of my list now is as follows:

1. _____

2. _____

3. _____

4. _____

5. _____

6. _____

(Continued)

7. _____

8. _____

9. _____

10. _____

11. _____

12. _____

13. _____

14. _____

15. _____

4. My five most important values are:

1. _____

   _____

2. _____

   _____

3. _____

   _____

4. _____

   _____

5. _____

   _____

MY VALUES–PART 3

■ **PURPOSE:** To prize your values and to identify potential rewards that can be used as motivators.

Use the space provided to list twenty activities that you love to do. These activities can be big or small, ones that you do indoors, outdoors, by yourself, or with others. Be specific when listing the activities (e.g., reading mystery novels). When you finish your list, complete the statements that follow.

Twenty Activities I Love To Do

1. _____
2. _____
3. _____
4. _____
5. _____
6. _____
7. _____
8. _____
9. _____
10. _____
11. _____
12. _____
13. _____
14. _____

(Continued)

15. _____

16. _____

17. _____

18. _____

19. _____

20. _____

Review your list of activities and then complete the following statements.

1. I have identified the following patterns in the activities that I love to do:

_____

_____

_____

_____

_____

_____

_____

2. The aspects that please me the most about this list are:

_____

_____

_____

_____

_____

_____

_____

3. From this exercise I learned the following about myself:

_____

_____

_____

_____

_____

4. Three values that are suggested by my list of activities are:

1. _____

2. _____

3. _____

5. Five activities on my list that I have not done within the last six months are:

1. _____

2. _____

3. _____

4. _____

5. _____

6. Five activities on my list that I can use as motivators for myself are:

1. _____

2. _____

3. _____

4. _____

5. _____

■ *PURPOSE:* To clarify and to prioritize your values.

Review the list of values you ranked in My Values—Part 2, Statement #3. Consider what you have learned about your values by completing these exercises. Then record in the following table your five most important values, your five somewhat important values, and your five least important values. You can use this rank-ordered list to remind yourself of your values and to use these values in making decisions.

Most Important

1. _____
2. _____
3. _____
4. _____
5. _____

Somewhat Important

1. _____
2. _____
3. _____
4. _____
5. _____

Least Important

1. _____
2. _____
3. _____
4. _____
5. _____

■ **PURPOSE:** To evaluate the consistency of the harmony between your actions and your values.

From the My Values—Part 4 exercise, record your five most important values. Then for the next week keep a written record of the actions you take to support your values. For example, if one of your Most Important Values is being helpful, you will record actions such as volunteering for a community-cleanup committee or sending a journal article to a colleague as actions during the week which support that value.

My Most Important Values Are:

1. _____

_____

_____

2. _____

_____

_____

3. _____

_____

_____

4. _____

_____

_____

5. _____

_____

_____

LOG

Day of the Week	My Value	My Action
Monday	_____	_____
	_____	_____
Tuesday	_____	_____
	_____	_____
Wednesday	_____	_____
	_____	_____
Thursday	_____	_____
	_____	_____
Friday	_____	_____
	_____	_____
Saturday	_____	_____
	_____	_____
Sunday	_____	_____
	_____	_____

DISCOVERING WHO YOU ARE: YOUR BELIEFS

You discovered that values are at the center of your thoughts and feelings about yourself and about life. Your values lead you to make decisions and to act in a certain way based on those thoughts and feelings. Growing from your values are attitudes about yourself, other people, situations, objects, or ideas. These attitudes are your beliefs. For example, if one of your values is being helpful or working for the welfare of others, you may believe that you should volunteer time to your community's food pantry.

Your beliefs have a powerful impact on your behavior. Although you may be unaware of this interplay, your beliefs—both positive and negative—affect how you behave. Negative beliefs such as "I can't do math," limit your behavior. If you truly believe that you can't do math, you don't put forth the needed effort to try to understand mathematical concepts, and as a result, you fail. In effect, the belief comes true because you believe it to be so. Psychologists call this a self-fulfilling prophecy.

Self-fulfilling prophecy works also with positive beliefs. In fact, positive beliefs are just as powerful as negative beliefs. The difference is that positive beliefs—"I can find a job I love," or "I can succeed in graduate school,"—spur you to action and stimulate you to make progress. They allow you to focus on an objective, take the steps needed to achieve that goal, and pursue that target with persistence and confidence.

You can harness the power of positive beliefs by using a technique called positive self-talk. This is a way to silence that negative inner voice that undermines your chances for success.

The niggling negative voice is like an audiotape, playing the same message over and over again on the tape player of your mind. Positive self-talk, also called affirmations, enables you to "erase" the old, negative messages and to "record" new, positive messages that you can listen to every day. The new messages use "I" statements in the present tense, focus on what could be, and include positive action: "I like who I am and the successful direction in which I'm headed." Since thought comes before action, affirmations ready your mind to create or attract circumstances that will help you reach your goals.

Use the following exercises to identify your negative beliefs, turn them into positive beliefs, and then use them as affirmations.

■ **PURPOSE:** To identify negative beliefs and to transform them into positive beliefs.

1. Use the space provided to list five negative beliefs you have about yourself that you think have affected your behavior. For example, "I am a boring person. No one would be interested in me."

    1. _____

    2. _____

    3. _____

    4. _____

    5. _____

2. Psychologist and philosopher William James recommended that: "If you want a quality, act as if you already had it." Use the space provided to rewrite your negative beliefs into positive beliefs. Remember to use "I" statements in the present tense, focus on what could be, and include positive action. For example, "I am an interesting person, and I look forward to meeting new people."

    1. _____

    2. _____

    3. _____

    4. _____

    5. _____

■ **PURPOSE:** To transform positive beliefs into affirmations and to put them into daily practice.

I. An easy way to begin using affirmations is to choose a simple aspect of your life that you would like to see changed. For example, "I have trouble finishing projects on time." In the following space, write one aspect of your life that you would like to see changed.

_____

_____

_____

_____

_____

_____

_____

2. Next, picture in your mind how you will act when you change this aspect of your life. Then, write an "I" statement that is positive, uses present tense, and focuses on the change. For example: "I enjoy finishing each project in a timely manner." In the following space, write your affirmation.

_____

_____

_____

_____

_____

_____

_____

3. Erasing negative mental messages requires repetition of the positive mental message. Choose one of these two methods: (1) write your affirmation on paper; (2) read your affirmation aloud. Then enact your chosen method at least ten times each day for the next two weeks. In the following space, write the method you plan to use.

_____

_____

_____

_____

_____

_____

_____

_____

4. At the end of two weeks, describe in the following space your experience with your affirmation. Did it change your actions? Compare how you felt two weeks ago and how you feel now.

_____

_____

_____

_____

_____

_____

_____

_____

_____

DISCOVERING WHO YOU ARE: YOUR SELF-BELIEF

You've identified your values and clarified your beliefs. The combination of your values and your beliefs is your self-belief. Psychologists define self-belief as a person's confidence in and respect for his or her own abilities. If you have a strong self-belief, you know who you are and what you value, and you can triumph over any adversity. Use the exercise on the following page to evaluate your self-belief.

■ **PURPOSE:** To describe your current self-belief and to envision your future self-belief.

Complete the following statements on your personality traits in the space provided. Personality traits include qualities such as being ambitious, considerate, gloomy, insensitive, motivated, outgoing, passive, quiet, etc.

1. Right now, I see myself as having the following personality traits:

_____

_____

_____

_____

_____

_____

_____

2. In the future, I hope to have the following personality traits:

_____

_____

_____

_____

_____

_____

_____

YOUR BASIS FOR SUCCESS

Your self-belief is your basis for success. Believing in yourself allows you to use all of your potential to take action. When you take action, you make progress and achieve results. Achieving results strengthens your self-belief because of the sense of accomplishment. With a strengthened self-belief, you gain the confidence to be bolder in your actions. Being bolder in your actions boosts your self-belief. You could think of this system as a power wheel with four linking components: potential leads to action, which leads to results, which leads to self-belief. Once you allow your power wheel to begin rolling, there's no telling what you can accomplish or where you can go.

DETERMINING WHAT YOU WANT TO ACCOMPLISH: YOUR DREAMS

Now that you've considered your values, beliefs, and self-beliefs, you have discovered who you are. The next step is to determine what you want to accomplish during your life. One way to do this is to think about your dreams.

What is your fondest dream? Do you long to launch your own business? Do you aspire to elected public office? Do you yearn to become a fashion designer? Spinning dreams is often called building castles in the air. Many people stop there, but successful people construct foundations for their dreams. You can do this, too. Complete the following exercise to get in touch with your deepest dreams and wishes.

MY DREAMS

■ **PURPOSE:** To identify your dreams and wishes.

1. Imagine that you have only one year left to live. Use the space provided to describe how you would spend those last 12 months.

_____

_____

_____

_____

_____

_____

2. A genie magically materializes before you and grants you three wishes. What do you wish for?

   1. _____

   2. _____

   3. _____

3. A wizard waves a magic wand and guarantees you success in anything you wish to do. What do you choose?

_____

_____

_____

_____

_____

(Continued)

4. Review your answers to the questions in this exercise. Do your answers reveal a pattern? Does a specific goal appear consistently among the three scenarios? What do you observe when you compare all of your answers? Note those observations in the space provided.

_____

_____

_____

_____

_____

_____

_____

_____

_____

_____

_____

_____

_____

_____

_____

_____

_____

_____

_____

_____

Determining What You Want To Accomplish: Your Goals

Your dreams can be the springboard for many of your goals, and goals come in various shapes and sizes. You probably have personal, educational, professional, and community goals. Within the scope of this book, you'll have an opportunity to concentrate on professional goals.

Professional goals are the objectives for your career. These objectives can be broad-based—"I want to earn a competitive wage,"—or narrowly focused—"I want to acquire a professional pilot's license."

In setting professional goals, strive to be realistic, considering your unique talents and attributes. For example, you may wish to be a dancer on Broadway. But if you have short legs and two left feet, your goal is unrealistic. You can waste much energy trying to reach an unrealistic goal, or you can channel that energy into another aspect of that goal, one that is more realistic for you.

In addition to making your goals realistic, you will want to be sure they'll take some effort to achieve. Easily attained goals that fail to challenge you don't allow you to reach your full potential.

Another consideration for the goals you set is the length of time required to achieve them. Short-term goals can be attained in one year or less. Intermediate-term goals can be attained in one to five years. Long-term goals can take five years or longer to attain.

The time commitment necessary for intermediate- and long-term goals often discourages people from setting any goals at all. This needn't happen to you, if you have the right mindset. For example, your long-term goal may be to earn a doctorate degree on a part-time basis, and you estimate that this will take ten years. Break down this long-term goal into a series of short-term goals. View each course you take as a short-term goal contributing to your long-term objective.

After you've thought about your professional goals, commit those goals to paper. Research shows that individuals who write out their goals are more likely to achieve them than people who fail to jot them down.

When recording your goals, bear in mind these strategies:

■ *Set a variety of realistic goals.* Having a number of goals with varying time commitments—short-term and long-term—in different areas of your life—personal, professional, educational—will allow you to maintain balance. But be realistic. Don't set so many goals that you become frustrated when you can't achieve them all.

■ *Choose goals that are yours.* Well-intentioned people in your life may encourage you to set goals that are unrealistic or just plain wrong for you. Make sure your goals spring from your dreams so that you'll feel satisfaction in achieving them.

■ *Use positive language.* Write "I will accept a job with a company that offers a mentoring program," rather than "I won't take a job unless the company offers a mentoring program."

■ *Be specific.* Write "I would like to visit Italy," rather than "I want to take a trip."

■ *Make your goals measurable.* You could write "I want to lose weight." But how will you know that you've attained your goal? After 5 pounds? After 25 pounds? You need a method by which you measure whether or not you've achieved your goal. You make your goals measurable when you answer these questions: What is to be accomplished? At what point will I know that I have accomplished it? "I want to lose 15 pounds," is a measurable goal.

■ *Establish a deadline.* What is the time frame for achieving your goal? Whether you want to attain the goal in six months or in six years, set a start date and an end date.

■ *Remember the nature of goals.* Your goals will change, so it's important to reassess your goals on a regular basis as you grow, change, and develop.

Use the exercise on the following two pages to identify your professional goals and the time commitments necessary for you to achieve them.

■ **PURPOSE:** To record your professional goals and to classify your goals as *short-term* (one year or less to accomplish), *intermediate-term* (one to five years to accomplish), or *long-term* (more than five years to accomplish). In the space provided, write up to five short-term, intermediate-term, and long-term goals.

Professional Goals
Short-Term

1. _____

   _____

2. _____

   _____

3. _____

   _____

4. _____

   _____

5. _____

   _____

Intermediate-Term

1. _____
   _____

2. _____
   _____

3. _____
   _____

4. _____
   _____

5. _____
   _____

Long-Term

1. _____
   _____

2. _____
   _____

3. _____
   _____

4. _____
   _____

5. _____
   _____

A head of you is a journey of a thousand miles. Since you want to arrive by the most direct route, you might consider using a map to lessen the chances of getting lost along the way. "Begin with the end in mind," according to Stephen R. Covey, the author of *The Seven Habits of Highly Effective People.* So after you've decided on your destination—your goal—create a map or an action plan to plot out exactly how you will arrive at your objective.

Reflect on a long-term goal first, stating your objective specifically and indicating a time frame for accomplishing it. Next, break down the long-term goal into a number of short-term goals—or steps—that will lead you to achieving the long-term objective. Monitor your progress by listing specific results of the short-term goals, then establish deadlines for each short-term goal.

Here's an example: Perhaps you want to open your own public relations firm, and you decide to accomplish this within seven years. With that in mind, you plan the various steps that you must take in order to launch the firm. The steps include: (1) gaining experience by working in a small public relations company for five years; (2) taking business courses at night to acquire accounting, management, and marketing skills; (3) saving 10 percent of your annual salary each year for five years to be used for start-up expenses; (4) obtaining a job after five years in a large public relations company to gain more specialized knowledge; and (5) saving 15 percent of your annual salary for the last two years to be used for living expenses after you open your firm.

In the exercise that follows, choose three of your most important long-term goals and create an action plan to help you achieve those goals.

■ *PURPOSE:* To focus on three important long-term goals and to create an action plan that leads to attainment of those goals.

1. Long-Term Goal: _____

To be accomplished by: _____

Step 1: _____

Results needed: _____

To be accomplished by: _____

Step 2: _____

Results needed: _____

To be accomplished by: _____

Step 3: _____

Results needed: _____

To be accomplished by: _____

Step 4: _____

Results needed: _____

To be accomplished by: _____

2. Long-Term Goal: _____

To be accomplished by: _____

Step 1: _____

Results needed: _____

To be accomplished by: _____

(Continued)

Step 2: _____

Results needed: _____

To be accomplished by: _____

Step 3: _____

Results needed: _____

To be accomplished by: _____

Step 4: _____

Results needed: _____

To be accomplished by: _____

3. Long-Term Goal: _____

To be accomplished by: _____

Step 1: _____

Results needed: _____

To be accomplished by: _____

Step 2: _____

Results needed: _____

To be accomplished by: _____

Step 3: _____

Results needed: _____

To be accomplished by: _____

Step 4: _____

Results needed: _____

To be accomplished by: _____

*O*nce you've completed your detailed action plan, you can begin your journey. The plan will keep you on track, but you must work hard to make progress, remain focused on your goals, and keep moving even when you encounter potholes and roadblocks.

Procrastination is one type of pothole. Rather than doing it now, a person puts off a task until later. That is the shortest route to failure. To overcome procrastination,

- *Set a start date.* This will allow you to get ready to begin once you have made a commitment to yourself.

- *Make a list of tiny tasks.* Tiny tasks take a mere minute or two, give you a sense of accomplishment, and enable you to begin.

- *Work for fifteen minutes.* Select a short period of time during each day when you accomplish tasks relating to your goal.

- *Tackle the hardest part first.* Once you have the hardest or the worst part behind you, the path to achieving the goal becomes smoother.

Chapter Five has other good tips about combating procrastination. If the pothole of procrastination doesn't stop you, the roadblock of fear sometimes does. Fear of failure or fear of success are both barriers to action.

Fear of failure often results when a person is afraid of appearing incompetent. The person views failure as defeat instead of considering that failure is only a temporary setback from which valuable lessons can be learned. According to psychologist B. F. Skinner, "A failure is not always a mistake, it may simply be the best one can do under the circumstances. The real mistake is to stop trying."

Fear of success often results when a person is afraid of new situations or responsibilities that success promises. The person views these changes as ones they don't deserve or ones they are incapable of handling. Successful writer, activist, and educator Audre Lorde believed that: "When I dare to be powerful—to use my strength in the service of my vision, then it becomes less and less important whether I am afraid."

To overcome fear,

- *Make a list of what makes you afraid.* Then create affirmations to counteract each item on your list.

- *Collect success stories.* Read about prominent people who experienced failure and from those stories study how those individuals rose above the failure and triumphed.

- *Write your own success stories.* Begin keeping a success journal, detailing each time you achieve something special, no matter how small. When you feel afraid, read through your journal and gain strength from the knowledge that, despite your fears, you are successful.

Maybe you are fortunate in not being halted by potholes and roadblocks as you follow your path to success. In fact, you may be chugging along at a good clip for a long stretch of time. Then, suddenly, you find yourself on a plateau with nothing much happening. The phenomenon of plateauing—making rapid progress then leveling out—is normal. Keep plugging away, and before you know it, you'll feel the beginnings of another spurt of progress.

To keep yourself going when you hit a plateau,

- *Keep your energy level high.* Repeat affirmations. Create special affirmations to help you cope with your plateau period. Practice visualization or the art of forming in your mind a picture of your goal. Visualize what it will be like when your goal is attained.

■ *Praise yourself.* Reflect on the distance you've already covered and congratulate yourself on your accomplishments.

■ *Reward yourself.* For each step toward a goal, treat yourself to something you enjoy. Use some of the motivators you discovered in the exercise *My Values— Part 3.*

■ *Share your successes with family and friends.* Tell the people in your life about your goals and what you have achieved so far. Not only will they congratulate you, but the pride reflected in their smiles and the good wishes they extend to you will act as powerful motivators to keep you going.

How Close Are You To Success?

According to Thomas Edison, "Many of life's failures are people who did not realize how close they were to success when they gave up." By monitoring the attainment of your short-term goals, you will know how close you are to successfully achieving your long-term goals. But keep in mind that circumstances sometimes cause goals to shift and to change. So you may find it helpful to obtain periodic feedback on the progress you are making. Use the following as a mechanism for action plan feedback.

ACTION PLAN FEEDBACK

■ *PURPOSE:* To obtain feedback and evaluation of strategies for attaining goals.

Periodically, check your progress along the path to evaluate how you are doing. This feedback will help you to know that either your action plan is progressing smoothly or you need to make course corrections. Focusing on one of your goals at a time, complete each statement using the space provided:

1. To date, I have accomplished:

_____

_____

_____

_____

_____

2. The parts I liked were:

_____

_____

_____

_____

3. The parts I didn't like were:

_____

_____

_____

_____

4. I forgot to include the following steps:

_____

_____

_____

_____

_____

_____

5. I will change or adjust the following:

_____

_____

_____

_____

_____

_____

6. Regarding the time frame, I need to make the following adjustment:

_____

_____

_____

_____

_____

_____

As you come to the end of this chapter, reflect on the journey of a thousand miles that you began with the process of self-discovery. You discovered who you are—your values, beliefs, and self-belief. You discovered what you want to accomplish—your dreams and goals. You created an action plan and learned how to follow the path to success by overcoming procrastination and fear and by keeping yourself going when you hit a plateau. You also discovered how to tell how close you are to the success you envision.

Don't stop there. Step into Chapter Two where you'll focus on success in the job search—your next step on your journey of a thousand miles.

Read All About It!

Bristol, Claude M. *The Magic of Believing: The Science of Setting Your Goal and Then Reaching It.* New York, NY: Simon & Schuster, 1992.

Carter, Carol, Gary Izumo, & Sarah Lyman Kravits. *The Career Tool Kit: Skills for Success.* Upper Saddle River, NJ: Prentice Hall Press, 1997.

Covey, Stephen R. *The Seven Habits of Highly Effective People.* New York, NY: Simon & Schuster, 1989.

Dean, Amy E., & Dan Olmos. *Lifegoals: Setting & Achieving Goals to Chart the Course of Your Life.* Carlsbad, CA: Hay House, 1991.

Driggers, Joann. *Life Management Skills: Taking Charge of Your Future.* Albany, NY: Delmar Publishers, 1999.

Gale, Linda. *Discover What You're Best At: A Complete Career System That Lets You Test Yourself To Discover Your Own True Career Capabilities.* New York, NY: Fireside, 1998.

Greeson, Gene. *Goal Setting: Turning Your Mountains Into Molehills.* St. Charles, MO: Potentials Unlimited, 1994.

Jarow, Rick. *Creating the Work You Love: Courage, Commitment and Career.* Rochester, VT: Inner Traditions International Ltd., 1995.

Leatz, Christine A., & Mary W. Stolar. *Career Success/Personal Success: How to Stay Healthy in a High Stress Environment.* New York, NY: McGraw-Hill, 1992.

Peale, Norman Vincent, & Kenneth Blanchard. *The Power of Ethical Management.* New York, NY: Fawcett, 1989.

Pitino, Rick, with Bill Reynolds. *Success Is A Choice: Ten Steps to Overachieving in Business and Life.* New York, NY: Broadway Books, 1997.

Rouillard, Larrie A. *Goals and Goal Setting.* Los Altos, CA: Crisp Publications, 1998.

Simon, Sidney, Leland W. Howe, & Howard Kirschenbaum. *Values Clarification: A Handbook of Practical Strategies for Teachers and Students.* Chesterfield, MA: Values Press, 1978.

Throop, Robert K., & Marion B. Castellucci. *Reaching Your Potential: Personal and Professional Development,* 2nd ed. Albany, NY: Delmar Publishers, 1999.

Waitley, Denis. *The New Dynamics of Goal Setting: Flextactics for a Fast-Changing Future.* New York, NY: William Morrow & Co., 1997.

Wilson, Susan B. *Goal Setting (The Worksmart Series).* New York, NY: AMACOM, 1994.

Books I've Read

Use the space provided to list the books you've read in this subject area and to reflect on what you've learned from reading them.

1. _____
2. _____
3. _____
4. _____
5. _____

Internet Resources

http://www.selfgrowth.com — **_Self-Improvement Online, Inc._** This Web site contains information on personal growth and provides links to other sites and newsgroups.

www.sncc.sk.ca/develop.html — **_New Careers On-line._** This Web site offers information on setting and achieving professional goals.

http://www.psych-web.com/mtsite/index.html — **_Mind Tools Ltd._** This British company offers software that helps people achieve more productive thinking. Their Web site contains general advice on goal setting and suggestions for achieving goals.

http://www.vgc.co.za/ — **_Virtual Global College._** This South African organization has a Web site that offers general goal-setting tips.

My Favorite Internet Sites

Use the space provided to list your favorite Internet sites.

1. _____

2. _____

3. _____

4. _____

5. _____

Career Success Notes

_____

_____

_____

_____

_____

_____

_____

_____

_____

_____

_____

_____

_____

_____

_____

_____

_____

_____

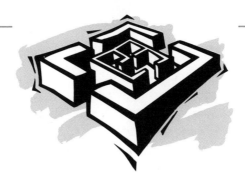

CHAPTER TWO

SUCCESS in the Job Search

Jobs don't find you. You find jobs. Find the right job successfully by setting a career objective; conducting a personalized job search complete with resumé, cover letter, and portfolio; and knowing how to attain and maintain a positive attitude. This chapter will help you to accomplish these vital tasks.

After completing this chapter, you should understand:

▪ how to match yourself to a career and set a career objective

▪ the components of a successful job search

▪ how to develop a personalized job search

▪ how to create a resumé, cover letter, and portfolio

▪ the strategies for keeping a positive mental attitude

Anthropologist Ashley Montagu said it in a nutshell: "It is work, work that one delights in, that is the surest guarantor of happiness." Wouldn't it be great to love your work? To use your abilities and interests to make a difference in the world? To be paid for doing a job that you're good at, a job that's fun?

> **Success doesn't come to you...you go to it.**
>
> MARVA COLLINS,
> AMERICAN EDUCATOR

A job? Fun? Yes! Knowing who you are and what you want to accomplish puts you on the fast track to challenging jobs and a satisfying career. Successful people know that work is play, and that's where the fun part comes in. No boring, dead-end jobs for you. By figuring out what you have to offer and what you want out of a career, you'll be able to find jobs that are good matches for you, pull together a resumé and cover letter, and launch a personalized search for the right job—one that delights you and makes you happy.

At the Crossroads of Success

You are at the crossroads of success. The next steps you take will mean the difference between a job that just pays the bills and a career that pays off by giving you more than just a salary.

Start by heading to your local library and looking at the *Occupational Outlook Handbook,* published by the U.S. Department of Labor's Bureau of Labor Statistics. You'll find information about employment trends, descriptions of hundreds of occupations, and sources of career guidance. You can also access *Occupational Outlook Handbook* on-line at http://stats.bls.gov (click on "Publications and Research Papers").

Find out if your library has the periodical *Occupational Outlook Quarterly,* also published by the U.S. Department of Labor. You'll find up-to-date information about job market trends and predictions about the fastest-growing jobs within the hottest industries.

Your library will also have resources about the educational requirements of various jobs. That information will help you decide if your current degree will open those job doors or if you'll be more successful by going to graduate school.

Once you've learned about the job market and educational requirements for jobs, you can match yourself to a career. That begins by looking at you—at your qualities and abilities.

MATCHING YOURSELF TO A CAREER

Many people who are still in college, newly graduated, or about to change careers often think they have no skills or abilities to offer prospective employers. They're wrong! You can prove it to yourself.

The U.S. Department of Labor compiled a list of personal qualities, foundation skills, and workplace skills that lead to top job performance in today's workplace. They apply to any type of career. For some jobs, though, you'll need more of some skills than others. How do you stack up? Scan the list and then complete the exercise that follows.

WHAT YOU NEED FOR TOP JOB PERFORMANCE TODAY[1]

PERSONAL QUALITIES

Individual responsibility

Self-belief

Self-management

Sociability

Integrity

FOUNDATION SKILLS

Basic Skills:

Reading

Writing

Arithmetic

Mathematics

Speaking

Listening

Thinking Skills:

Ability to learn

Reasoning

Creative thinking

Decision Making

Problem solving

RESOURCE SKILLS

Allocate time, money, materials, space, and staff

INTERPERSONAL SKILLS

Work on teams
Teach others
Serve customers
Lead
Negotiate
Work with people of diverse backgrounds

INFORMATION SKILLS

Acquire and evaluate data
Organize and maintain files
Interpret and communicate
Use computers to process information

SYSTEMS SKILLS

Understand social, organizational, and technological systems
Monitor and correct performance
Design or improve systems

TECHNOLOGY SKILLS

Select equipment and tools
Apply technology to specific tasks
Maintain and troubleshoot equipment

[1]Source: U.S. Department of Labor, Secretary's Commission on Achieving Necessary Skills (SCANS), *Learning a Living: A Blueprint for High Performance,* Washington, DC, 1992, page 3.

■ **PURPOSE:** To identify your skills and abilities.

1. For this exercise, refer to your answers in *My Values—Part 3*. What are the five activities you most enjoy doing? Choose from those you enjoy at work or at school, at home or in the community, during sports or recreation.

1. _____

_____

2. _____

_____

3. _____

_____

4. _____

_____

5. _____

_____

2. Refer to the skills listed in the exercise *What You Need for Top Job Performance Today*. Think about how you use those skills in the five activities you most enjoy doing. List those skills in the space provided.

Skills I Enjoyed Using in Activity #1

_____

_____

_____

_____

_____

Skills I Enjoyed Using in Activity #2

_____

_____

_____

_____

_____

Skills I Enjoyed Using in Activity #3

_____

_____

_____

_____

_____

Skills I Enjoyed Using in Activity #4

_____

_____

_____

_____

_____

Skills I Enjoyed Using in Activity #5

_____

_____

_____

_____

_____

(Continued)

3. Go back to the list in the exercise *What You Need for Top Job Performance Today*. Circle all the qualities and skills that you just listed for each activity. How do you stack up? Write your answer in the space provided.

_____

_____

_____

_____

_____

_____

_____

_____

_____

_____

_____

_____

_____

_____

_____

_____

_____

_____

_____

_____

_____

_____

Beside qualities and skills, you also have education and experience to offer prospective employers. Your education shows that you have the ability to learn and demonstrates that you can read, write, and do computations. It also points to the body of knowledge you've gained in specific areas such as accounting, management, or computer information systems.

Your work experience is valuable, too. This includes:

▪ full-time or part-time paid work

▪ apprenticeships and internships

▪ community, church, or other volunteer work

Even if the job is occasional or unpaid, every work experience brings the chance to develop important skills that are valued in the workplace.

A prospective employer looks at your qualities, skills, education, and experience to determine if you would be a good match for a job. At the same time, you need to consider certain factors about the company or the job that are important to you. These factors will help you to focus your job search in areas of work that would be a good match for you. Use the exercise that follows to think about what you want from a career.

WHAT I WANT FROM MY CAREER

■ **PURPOSE:** To identify the elements of a job that are most important to you.

For sections 1 through 10, check all that apply.

1. I prefer to work most with:

   ____ resources (e.g., environment, money, employees, etc.)

   ____ people (e.g., children, peers, the elderly, the poor, etc.)

   ____ information (e.g., visuals, numbers, words, etc.)

   ____ systems (e.g., social groups, work processes, information systems, etc.)

   ____ technology (e.g., computers, cooking equipment, hand tools, machinery, etc.)

2. The types of *resources* I would most enjoy working with are:

   ____ the environment

   ____ money

   ____ employees

   ____ equipment

   ____ other: _____

3. The types of *people* I would most enjoy working with are:

   ____ children

   ____ peers

   ____ the elderly

   ____ the poor

   ____ other: _____

4. The types of *information* I would most enjoy working with are:

_____ Internet

_____ numbers

_____ visuals

_____ words

_____ other: _____

5. The types of *systems* I would most enjoy working with are:

_____ social groups

_____ work processes

_____ information systems

_____ communication systems

_____ other: _____

6. The types of *technology* I would most enjoy working with are:

_____ computers

_____ cooking equipment

_____ hand tools

_____ machinery

_____ other: _____

7. The area(s) of the country in which I would like to work is/are:

_____ North

_____ Northeast

_____ Southeast

_____ South

_____ Midwest

_____ West

_____ Northwest

_____ Southwest

(Continued)

8. I would like to work in:

_____ urban areas

_____ suburban areas

_____ rural areas

9. I would like to work:

_____ indoors

_____ outdoors

10. I would like to work in:

_____ a casual work environment

_____ a formal work environment

11. I would like to work for:

_____ a large corporation

_____ a small company

_____ my own business

For sections 12 through 14, complete the statement.

12. The values that are important for me in my work are:

_____

_____

_____

_____

13. The amount of job security (e.g., short-term job or long-term job) I need is:

_____

_____

_____

_____

14. The amount of salary I want is:

_____

_____

_____

_____

SETTING A CAREER OBJECTIVE

So far you've looked at the employment market and educational requirements for various jobs. You know your qualities, skills, and experiences plus the factors about the company or job that are important to you. Now comes the exciting part—you're ready to combine this research and thinking to come up with one or two occupations as your career objective. Having a career objective will guide your job search and make it easier for you to find a job you will enjoy. Use the following exercise to set your career objective.

■**PURPOSE:** To identify a career objective. (Note: *The Occupational Outlook Handbook* is an ideal resource for this exercise.)

1. List all of the occupations that appeal to you.

_____

_____

_____

_____

_____

2. List three occupations that are the most interesting to you.

1. _____

2. _____

3. _____

3. Choose one or two occupations that are the best match for you in terms of your skills or interests.

_____

_____

_____

4. State the goal you have for your career.

_____

_____

_____

My career objective is:

_____

_____

_____

COMPONENTS OF A SUCCESSFUL JOB SEARCH

*H*aving a career objective means you can now plan your job search. Job hunting is hard work, and a successful job search involves a number of tasks:

1. Preparing your resumé

2. Obtaining references/letters of recommendation

3. Finding job openings through:

    a. people you know

    b. employers

    c. college placement offices

    d. internships and job shadowing

    e. career fairs

    f. classified ads

    g. private employment agencies

    h. government employment services

    i. job clearinghouses

    j. the Internet

4. Writing cover letters

5. Preparing a portfolio

6. Completing employment applications

7. Interviewing

8. Assessing job offers

9. Declining/accepting offers

CONDUCTING A SUCCESSFUL JOB SEARCH

*B*ecause job-hunting is tough, the first step in launching a successful job search is having the right attitude. You may be lucky enough to find the right job within a few days. Or you may have to hunt for weeks or months before clicking with the best opportunity. A lengthy job search can chip away at your self-belief and self-confidence, especially if you face a lot of rejection and disappointment. Don't let this affect your attitude!

Motivate yourself to keep moving forward. Reward yourself after you send out a round of resumés. Congratulate yourself when an interview appointment comes through for you. Use positive self-talk to reaffirm what you have to offer to prospective employers. Practice visualization. Picture yourself at the job of your dreams, working with colleagues, accomplishing goals, winning praise from the boss. Keeping these images in your mind will help you to overcome the discouragement that is a part of almost every job search.

The next step is planning and organizing your job search. Begin your job search with a plan for tasks 1 through 6 of the process listed previously. Use the form *My Job Search Plan* to build your plan, highlight the steps of each task, and set goals for the completion of the tasks.

MY JOB SEARCH PLAN

Task: _____

    Step 1: _____

    Results needed: _____

    To be accomplished by: _____

Task: _____

    Step 2: _____

    Results needed: _____

    To be accomplished by: _____

Task: _____

    Step 3: _____

    Results needed: _____

    To be accomplished by: _____

Task: _____

    Step 4: _____

    Results needed: _____

    To be accomplished by: _____

Task: _____

    Step 5: _____

    Results needed: _____

    To be accomplished by: _____

(Continued)

Task: _____

Step 6: _____

Results needed: _____

To be accomplished by: _____

Make photocopies of *My Job Search Plan* and place them either in a three-ring binder or a two-pocket folder. This becomes your job search notebook. Think of this tool as job-search central because it will organize all of the details of your job hunt for easy reference and effective follow-up.

Other forms to include in your job search notebook are the following *My Job Search Notes,* and the *Interview Notes* included at the end of this journal. Prepare one page for each company you contact and arrange the pages in your notebook in alphabetical order by company name.

MY JOB SEARCH NOTES

Company: _____

Contact: _____

Contact's title: _____

Address: _____

Telephone: _____

Fax: _____

E-mail: _____

Referred by: _____

Initial contact _____

    Letter or phone? _____ Date: _____

    Result: _____

Follow-up #1

    Letter or phone? _____ Date: _____

    Result: _____

Follow-up #2

    Letter or phone? _____ Date: _____

    Result: _____

Resumé submitted

    ❑ Yes   ❑ No   Date: _____

    Result: _____

(Continued)

First interview

    Date: _____

    Result: _____

    Thank-you note sent: _____

Second Interview

    Date: _____

    Result: _____

    Thank-you note sent: _____

Comments:

_____

_____

_____

_____

_____

_____

_____

_____

_____

_____

_____

When your job search is planned and organized, your next step is to research prospective employers offering the kinds of jobs that meet your career objective. Compile a list of companies by consulting the telephone company's Yellow Pages and directories of local Chambers of Commerce and trade associations, which are available at the library. Then request information about the company from its public relations department, check your public library for business indexes such as *Thomas Register*, or download information from the company's Internet Web site. For each company that appeals to you, find the answers to the following questions:

■ What does the company sell or produce?

■ Is the company small or large?

■ Is the company a for-profit or not-for-profit enterprise?

■ What is the company's reputation in the community and in the industry?

■ What are the company's problems?

Record your findings on the following form *My Prospective Employer Research* and include a form for each company in your job search notebook. Compiling this information will help you formulate questions to ask during your interview.

Company: _____

Address: _____

Telephone: _____

Fax: _____

E-mail: _____

This company's recent products, services, or ventures are:

_____

_____

_____

This company is: ❑ Small   ❑ Large

Number of employees: _____

This company is   ❑ For-Profit   ❑ Non-Profit

This company's financial status/earnings profile is: _____

_____

_____

_____

This company's reputation in the community is: _____

_____

_____

_____

This company's reputation in the industry is: _____

_____

_____

_____

_____

This company's problems are: _____

_____

_____

_____

_____

Comments: _____

_____

_____

_____

_____

_____

_____

_____

_____

_____

_____

_____

_____

_____

_____

Nancy Link

Vice President, Thomson University, ITP

In her position as Vice President, Thomson University at ITP, Nancy Link sees dozens of job candidates coming right out of college and wanting to work for International Thomson Publishing. She has hired straight-A students and those who've pulled Bs and Cs. Grades aren't all that important to Link. Instead, she looks for special qualities in the candidate.

"I look for somebody who's got a personality, who's got passion about something, who has something to give," Link says. "Give me someone who can show me that he or she is going to work hard, that he or she is going to get excited, that the person is going to come to me and ask for help and guidance."

Link feels an admiration for people who do whatever it takes to land that first job, including working at paid or unpaid internships, going through a temporary placement agency, or taking another job with the company. "This is not only creative, it's also giving you more experience, so why not go for it?" Link says.

> **We have a lot to get done here and I want to hire someone who not only has the skills and abilities to do it, but they've got it in their heart to get it done too. The head has to balance out with the heart.**

"I think if people find a company that they want to work for, they'll do almost any job in order to get into the company. I see that a lot at ITP. They'll do whatever it takes to find a home here. That shows me they'll be committed to the company."

That show of commitment is often enough to get an interview with Link. What does she look for in the candidate at that point? Link looks for someone who asks questions about the business: how the company is structured, who the competitors are, how bright is the company's future, what is the career ladder for the position the person is interested in.

"Show me you're interested in the business. That will show me that you have the heart, that you've got that fire in your belly, and it also tells me that you're not going to stick to whatever job duties are in that job description. You're willing to do whatever it takes because you care about the business moving forward, not just what's in it for you."

Once your company research is underway, you next need to hone your networking (see Chapter Four for a complete discussion of networking) and telephone techniques.

Networking involves spreading the word to everyone you know about the job you seek and the qualifications you offer. Start with family and friends then extend your networking efforts to the managers and executives you meet who can refer you to others in a position to hire.

Networking techniques involve good interpersonal skills—shaking hands, maintaining eye contact, smiling—combined with stating the job title or providing a brief description of your desired position, and letting the person know how you can be reached. Have a supply of business cards printed with your telephone number and e-mail address. Have printed on the back of the card a mini resumé, listing your top skills and attributes. Exchange business cards with those you meet. You never know how your business card will spread the word about your career objective, your skills, and your abilities.

In addition to developing solid networking skills, you'll need to practice effective telephone techniques until they become second nature to you.

Stand when you make a phone call. This allows you to project a strong, confident voice. Greet the person who answers the call, state your name, the name of the person you wish to speak to, and the reason for your call. For example, "Good morning! This is Peter Hess. I'd like to speak with Mr. Anderson please regarding a job opening." Courtesy and respect for those on the other end of the line will pay dividends as will a smile. True, your smile cannot be seen, but it can be heard because smiling affects your speech quality.

If you feel nervous speaking on the phone, take a few deep breaths before you punch in the number. Visualize the person on the other end of the line smiling when your call comes in and greeting you warmly. If you fear you'll become tongue-tied or forget what you want to say, write out a short script. Practice the script a few times so that you sound natural. You don't want to sound as if you're reciting canned language. (Chapter Five has other good tips on using the telephone.)

Networking and telephone techniques will help you get to an interview. What you wear to an interview often means the difference between getting the job or losing your chances. Research shows that a person's appearance is more important to an observer than a person's voice or words. Since you have only ten seconds to make a good first impression, make the most of that initial encounter.

Part of creating that good first impression is the way you dress. Dress standards have changed in the last few years. In many companies, the button-downed look has given way to casual business attire. How will you know what to wear?

One way to determine proper attire for an interview is to go to the prospective employer and park outside the building. Observe the clothing worn by the employees as they enter and leave the building. Be careful not to do this on a holiday or a Friday because many organizations have dress-down policies in effect on these days.

What do you see? People in suits? Women in mix-and-match skirts and blouses? Men in open-necked shirts and casual trousers? Use your observations to decide how button-downed or casual you should go. When in doubt, choose the traditional suit because it's better to be overdressed than underdressed. Whatever you wear, make sure your clothing is clean and pressed to make that first impression a good one. (Chapter Five has suggestions on putting together a working wardrobe.)

DEVELOPING A PERSONALIZED JOB SEARCH

*S*ome job seekers leave no stone unturned in their quest for employment. They attack the search with the entire arsenal of strategies from answering classified ads to cold calling prospective employers. Others prefer to focus their efforts, using only three or four different strategies. Develop your own personalized job search by choosing all or some of the following strategies from the job-seeker's arsenal.

1. *Networking With People You Know.* Many jobs aren't advertised in the Sunday classifieds. Instead they're advertised person to person. To tap into these unadvertised openings, network with people you know. Tell relatives, friends, other students, instructors, and colleagues about the type of job you seek and what you can offer a prospective employer. Ask for leads to jobs that might be of interest. Research shows that nearly 50 percent of all successful job seekers found their jobs by networking with people they know.

2. *Cold Calling Prospective Employers.* Cold calling is a basic technique used in sales. Since you are "selling" yourself to a prospective employer, cold calling works for job seekers, too. Here's how it works. You choose a prospective employer and arrive unannounced, asking to speak with someone about opportunities in the company. If you promise to take only five minutes of the person's time, you usually can get in. This gives you the chance to make a face-to-face contact and to leave your resumé and portfolio in the event that openings are available. Be aware that cold calling prospective employers is a controversial tactic. Some employers are turned off by this; others are not.

3. *Securing Information Interviews.* You make an appointment for an information interview. But instead of applying for a job, you seek information and advice from an industry expert about the field. Information interviews expand your employer research, multiply your networking contacts, and provide objective feedback from the expert on your qualifications.

4. *Registering With College Placement Offices.* Most colleges have job referral services for students and alumni. To tap into this source of job leads, you register by completing an application and including a copy of your resumé, your portfolio, and letters of recommendation. Some referral services match you to employers with openings, while others give you access to a job hot-line that you use to match yourself to prospective employers.

5. *Becoming an Intern/Participating In Job Shadowing.* Participating in an internship is an excellent way to gain real-life experience—and possibly a job—in a career field you are considering. Internships work well for the company, too. Companies often use their college intern programs as a source for new hires. Seeing how you work and interact as a team member allows a company to judge your effectiveness and potential as an employee.

   Job shadowing is another great way to experience a job firsthand. You spend a few hours or a day following or shadowing someone in your chosen occupation. This gives you a better idea of the ins and outs of a particular job and whether the occupation would be a good match for you. Ask those you know about becoming their shadow-for-the-day or check with your college placement office about putting you together with an appropriate person.

6. *Attending Career Fairs.* Companies send recruiters to career fairs with one goal—to find qualified people for

job vacancies. You will have assembled before you a host of potential employers, giving you the opportunity to interview them. Since a career fair is an interview opportunity, the company is looking you over, too, so be sure you dress appropriately for the big day.

Review the list of companies that will be present at the career fair, checking all the ones that interest you. Then prioritize the companies you've selected with #1 representing the company that holds the highest interest for you, #2 representing the company that holds the next highest interest for you, etc. Plan to visit the companies in prioritized order.

Many large career fairs offer maps so you can locate the exhibit areas of the particular companies in which you are interested. Find your target companies on the map and indicate next to the company's name the ranking on your prioritized list. This allows you to not only visualize the stops you'll be making but to cluster visits if several target companies are located in the same area.

If the first company on your list is swamped with job seekers, move on to the second company on your list. But don't forget to go back to Company #1. Cross off each company on your list after you've completed your visit.

At each company's exhibit area, introduce yourself to the recruiter and present your business card. Ask questions about the opportunities available at the company, take notes, and be prepared to speak about your accomplishments and goals. Above all, if the company and the job opportunities interest you, be sure to tell the recruiter how you see yourself as a good match for the company. Ask the recruiter if he or she would accept a copy of your resumé right then and there or if the recruiter would prefer that you mail or e-mail the resumé to the company.

7. *Answering Classified Ads.* Daily and Sunday local newspapers and professional and trade publications are

filled with hundreds of classified ads for jobs. Set up a consistent routine of checking these periodicals. Respond promptly to any ad that attracts you, and keep a record of every ad you answer.

8. *Registering With Private Employment Agencies.* Private employment agencies can offer temporary jobs, permanent jobs in general fields, temporary or permanent jobs in specialized areas, or executive-level positions. Registering with a private employment agency requires completing an application. Getting a job through a private employment agency requires either the employer or you to pay a fee for the service. Fees are usually a percentage of your first year's salary. Ask whether the employer or you will pay the fee and understand the financial arrangements before you use a private employment agency to find a job.

9. *Accessing Government Employment Services.* Most states have a job service that offers free referrals to local and statewide jobs. Check with your state's Department of Labor for information about these referrals. Look in the phone book for the number of the Department of Labor, visit their Web site, or check with your local library. Some libraries have a job service computer database that you can use.

10. *Registering With Job Clearinghouses.* Federal, private, and specialized job clearinghouses collect and distribute employment information such as job openings posted by employers and job qualifications posted by job seekers. Check with your local library for information about registering with national and statewide job clearinghouses.

11. *Tapping Into Internet Resources.* More than 11,000 Web sites post job openings. That includes corporate Web sites, college placement offices with on-line capability, local newspapers that publish an electronic version of

the paper, and state and federal employment agencies that maintain job databases. For example, the Young Adult Professional Associates, Inc., or YAPA®, Web site offers comprehensive services, including one-year free resumé posting; a YAPA® mailbox to collect all job matches; automatic e-mail messaging system that lets you know you have job matches in your YAPA® mailbox; ability to screen job matches, create personalized cover letters, build a resumé, and attach a portfolio to your resumé; ability to conduct a job or company search; plus the opportunities to participate in live chat-room discussions, an on-line mentor matching system, and a networking board to trade information and tips for success with other YAPA® members.

Consider posting your resumé on www.yapa.com for a free 30-day trial membership. During that trial period, you will receive direct job matches, and you can conduct a search of the companies using the site. (This trial membership can be used only once and does not include access to any of the other features on the site.)

You can also use the Internet to establish a personal home page. But keep in mind that not every employer uses the Internet. Tapping into Internet resources should not be your only job-hunting strategy.

Focus your personalized job search by completing the following exercise.

■**PURPOSE:** To identify strategies you will use in your job search.

1. The strategies I will use for my job search are: (Check all that apply.)

_____ Networking with people I know

_____ Cold calling prospective employers

_____ Securing informational interviews

_____ Registering with college placement offices

_____ Becoming an intern

_____ Participating in job shadowing

_____ Attending career fairs

_____ Answering classified ads

_____ Registering with private employment agencies

_____ Accessing government employment services

_____ Registering with job clearinghouses

_____ Tapping into Internet resources

2. Prioritize the strategies identified in #1. Place a (1) before the strategy that is most effective for your circumstances, a (2) before the strategy that is the next most effective, and so on.

3. My top five job search strategies are:

1. _____

2. _____

3. _____

4. _____

5. _____

Complete a *My Job Search Plan* form for each of your top five strategies. Place these forms in your job-search notebook.

Writing Your Resumé

Your resumé is a snapshot of your experience and qualifications. Most resumés usually contain the following:

- your name, address, telephone number, and e-mail address

- your career objective (optional)

- summary of your qualifications

- your education (i.e., names and locations of schools attended, dates of attendance, type of program, diploma or degree received)

- your work experience, including internships and community volunteer positions. Include the job title, name and location of the employer, and dates of employment.

- professional licenses

- your military experience (i.e., branch, length of service, major responsibilities, special training)

- your membership in organizations

- any special skills, honors, awards, or achievements

- information about the availability of references

Since presenting a career objective is optional, you'll need to think carefully about whether you'll include one or not. Many human resource directors believe that stating a career objective limits new college graduates.

Maybe your objective states: "Entry-level sales position with the potential for growth and advancement." Wanting a job that offers growth and advancement is almost a given. This doesn't tell the human resource director anything new. Additionally, if the company to which you've applied has current openings only in public relations or marketing, your resumé will go in the "no" pile.

New college graduates who hope to get a foot in the door are better off not including an objective on their resumés. Those who have more experience and more career focus should consider including a career objective.

You can arrange the information on your resumé in one of three popular formats:

■ chronological format

■ functional format

■ combination format

The chronological format (see page 80) lists your most recent job first, and then your other jobs in reverse chronological order. This is the most common format for a resumé.

The functional format (see page 81) transforms your work experience into functions and skills. If you are a career changer or someone with little or no formal work experience, this is an ideal format for you.

The combination format (see page 82) lists your functions and skills and shows your job history in reverse chronological order.

Use the following data sheet to compile the information you will use in your resumé.

Name: _____

Address: _____

Telephone Number: _____ E-mail: _____

Career Objective: _____

_____

My Qualifications: _____

_____

Education

College or Other Postsecondary School #1: _____

Address: _____

Date Started: _____ Date Ended: _____

Years Completed or Degree Received: _____ Course of Study: _____

Courses Relevant to Career Objective: _____

_____

Honors: _____

_____

Extracurricular Activities: _____

_____

College or Other Postsecondary School #2: _____

Address: _____

Date Started: _____ Date Ended: _____

(Continued)

Years Completed or Degree Received: _____ Course of Study: _____

Courses Relevant to Career Objective: _____

_____

Honors: _____

_____

Extracurricular Activities: _____

_____

High School _____

Address: _____

Date Started: _____ Date Ended: _____

Years Completed or Degree Received: _____ Course of Study: _____

Courses Relevant to Career Objective: _____

_____

Honors: _____

_____

Extracurricular Activities: _____

_____

Work Experience

Job Title: _____

Employer's Name and Address: _____

Supervisor's Name: _____

Date Started: _____ Date Ended: _____

Description of Responsibilities and Skills Used:

_____

_____

_____

_____

Job Title: _____

Employer's Name and Address: _____

Supervisor's Name: _____

Date Started: _____ Date Ended: _____

Description of Responsibilities and Skills Used:

_____

_____

_____

_____

Job Title: _____

Employer's Name and Address: _____

Supervisor's Name: _____

Date Started: _____ Date Ended: _____

Description of Responsibilities and Skills Used:

_____

_____

_____

_____

(Continued)

Professional Licenses

Name/Number of License: _____

Licensing Agency: _____

Military Experience

Rank: _____ Branch of Service: _____

Date Started: _____ Date Ended: _____

Description of Responsibilities and Skills Used:

Date Started: _____ Date Ended: _____

Description of Responsibilities and Skills Used:

_____

_____

_____

_____

Special Training: _____

_____

Personal Data

Awards, Honors, and Special Achievements: _____

_____

_____

Hobbies and Special Interests: _____

_____

_____

Foreign Languages

Organizations and Offices Held: _____

_____

_____

Volunteer Work: _____

_____

_____

_____

References

Educational Reference: _____

Name and Title: _____

Address: _____

Phone: _____

Educational Reference: _____

Name and Title: _____

Address: _____

Phone: _____

Character Reference: _____

Name and Title: _____

Address: _____

Phone: _____

Jesse Three Crows

23 First Street ■ Albany, NY 12208

(518) 555-3647 ■ jthreecrows@aol.com

WORK EXPERIENCE:

September 1992 to Present

Assistant Bookkeeper, Achievement Office Sales/Service, Albany, NY. Aid in bookkeeping, payroll services, and tax preparation.

September 1993 to May 1994

Internship at Goldworthy & Ames Certified Public Accountants, Albany, NY. Provided tax preparation assistance for five major clients.

September 1991 to April 1992

Tutor, Teaching and Learning Center, The College of Saint Rose, Albany, NY. Provided tutoring assistance in Math 121, 122 and Statistics I and II to students on an individual basis.

May 1990 to September 1994

Groundskeeper. Albany High School, Albany, NY. Maintained school grounds during summer break.

EDUCATION:

September 1990 to May 1994

The College of Saint Rose, Albany, NY
Bachelor of Science degree in Business Administration conferred in May 1994
Accounting GPA: 3.8
Overall GPA: 3.5

COMPUTER SKILLS:

Excel, Lotus 1-2-3, Word Perfect, Microsoft Word, IBM and Apple applications

LEADERSHIP EXPERIENCES:

Supervisor and team leader of client audits
Co-captain 1989-1990 State Championship basketball team
Two gold medals and one bronze—Team Handball—Empire State Games

REFERENCES:

Available upon request.

Resumé Sample: Functional Format

Jesse Three Crows

23 First Street ■ Albany, NY 12208

(518) 555-3647 ■ jthreecrows@aol.com

SKILLS / ACHIEVEMENTS: Supervisor and team leader of client audits

Excellent computer skills, including Excel, Lotus 1-2-3, Word Perfect, Microsoft Word, IBM and Apple applications.

Working with clients and interpreting their needs.

Working under the pressure of deadlines.

EMPLOYMENT HISTORY: Assistant Bookkeeper, Achievement Office Sales/Service, Albany, NY. 1992 to present.

Intern, Goldworthy & Ames Certified Public Accountants, Albany, NY. 1993 to 1994.

Tutor, Teaching and Learning Center, The College of Saint Rose, Albany, NY. 1991 to 1992.

Groundskeeper, Albany High School, Albany, NY. 1990 to 1994.

EDUCATION: Bachelor of Science degree, Business Administration, The College of Saint Rose, Albany, NY, May 1994.

RELEVANT COURSES: Financial Accounting, Behavioral Science in Business, Urban Economics, Managerial Economics, Financial Information Systems, Taxation, Strategic Marketing Planning, Investment Theory, New Business Ventures and the Entrepreneur, Performance and Financial Auditing

REFERENCES: Available upon request.

Resumé Sample: Combination Format

Jesse Three Crows

23 First Street ■ Albany, NY 12208

(518) 555-3647 ■ jthreecrows@aol.com

SKILLS / ACHIEVEMENTS: Supervisor and team leader of client audits

Excellent computer skills, including Excel, Lotus 1-2-3, Word Perfect, Microsoft Word, IBM and Apple applications.

Working with clients and interpreting their needs.

Working under the pressure of deadlines.

WORK EXPERIENCE:

September 1992 to Present   Assistant Bookkeeper, Achievement Office Sales/Service, Albany, NY. Aid in bookkeeping, payroll services, and tax preparation.

September 1993 to May 1994   Internship at Goldworthy & Ames Certified Public Accountants, Albany, NY. Provided tax preparation assistance for five major clients.

September 1991 to April 1992   Tutor, Teaching and Learning Center, The College of Saint Rose, Albany, NY. Provided tutoring assistance in Math 121, 122 and Statistics I and II to students on an individual basis.

May 1990 to September 1994   Groundskeeper. Albany High School, Albany, NY. Maintained school grounds during summer break.

EDUCATION:

September 1990 to May 1994   The College of Saint Rose, Albany, NY
Bachelor of Science degree in Business Administration conferred in May 1994
Accounting GPA: 3.8
Overall GPA: 3.5

REFERENCES: Available upon request.

RESUMÉ REQUIREMENTS

No matter which format you choose, keep your resumé to one page, unless you have extensive work experience to cite. Prepare your resumé on white or ivory bond paper with at least one-inch margins all around.

Describe your skills and abilities in short phrases instead of full sentences and use action words to describe your accomplishments. Avoid using humor, which almost always falls flat, and be truthful in everything you list on the resumé.

Have the content well organized, make sure your resumé looks neat, and that it's free of grammar and spelling errors. Don't trust your word processor's grammar- and spelling-check programs to find your mistakes! Eyeball the resumé yourself or ask someone with experience to edit and proof the resumé for you.

OBTAINING REFERENCES AND LETTERS OF RECOMMENDATION

As you create your resumé, think about people who would be willing to vouch for you as a reference or who would be willing to write a letter of recommendation. Select three or four people who know you well and who can comment positively about your work habits, skills, and personal qualities. Instructors, coaches, and job supervisors are good choices because they can be objective. Relatives and friends aren't good choices for obvious reasons. Nobody ever got a job because of praise from his or her mother.

Ask your potential references if they feel they could write a strong recommendation. Choose only those who can provide this for you. To make the task easier for your references, provide a copy of your resumé or other information about your direction and background.

The people you choose as references should be available by telephone when a prospective employer calls. If a person isn't easily available by telephone, ask the person to provide a letter of recommendation. A letter of recommendation offers a written appraisal of your work habits, skills, and personal qualities. Ask the person to address the letter To Whom It May Concern so that you can use the letter over and over again. You can also ask your college placement office to keep letters of recommendation on file for you.

WRITING COVER LETTERS

When you answer a classified job ad or another job listing, you send a copy of your resumé along with a one-page cover letter. Your cover letter shows your particular interest in a specific job, highlights your experience or skills, and gets the employer to read your resumé and to call you for an interview.

Cover letters must be individually tailored to each job posting you respond to. Here's a formula for can-do cover letters:

- Address your cover letter to a specific person, if possible, and make sure you spell the person's name correctly.

- Use the first paragraph to indicate the purpose of the letter. Note the job you are applying for and where you learned about the opening. If you were referred to the company, mention the name of the person who made the referral.

- Use the second paragraph to show why and how your skills and experience would be assets to the company.

- Use the third paragraph to ask for an interview and to tell the employer how you can be reached.

Since your cover letter will contribute to the employer's first impression of you, use a positive, upbeat tone and be certain that the cover letter is like the resumé—well-organized, neat, and free from errors. A sample cover letter is below.

Jesse Three Crows

23 First Street ■ Albany, NY 12208

(518) 555-3647 ■ jthreecrows@aol.com

January 15, 1999

Ms. Amee Wong
Human Resources Manager
Cutler & Quigley, Inc.
35 South Hills Road
Clifton Park, NY 12065

Dear Ms. Wong:

I am applying for the position of assistant accountant that was advertised in the January 14, 1999 edition of the Albany *Times Union*. My resumé is enclosed.

I am currently employed as an assistant bookkeeper at Achievement Office Sales/Service in Albany where I aid in bookkeeping, payroll services, and tax preparation. I have excellent computer skills and interact well with clients. I believe that my skills, experience, and motivation will benefit Cutler & Quigley, Inc.

I will be happy to make an appointment for an interview. You can reach me at 555-3647. I will plan to call you on January 23 to answer any questions you may have.

Sincerely,

Jesse Three Crows

enclosure

PREPARING A PORTFOLIO

While your cover letter and resumé get your foot in the door, a portfolio often clinches the deal. A portfolio is a collection of documents showing proof of your accomplishments, performance, and work history. You can include some or all of the following:

- an unofficial copy of your college transcript, showing your courses, number of credits, and letter grades

- a list of courses you are currently taking

- certificates of achievement that you received for volunteering in the community, attaining the dean's list, for completing a self-improvement workshop or for courses you've taken in Microsoft Word, Excel, Access, or PowerPoint.

- letters of recommendation

- projects you completed at work or at school that showcase your highest skill level. You could include written papers from a course in which you excelled, brochures you created at work, copies of your action plans showing proof that you've implemented the various steps.

Package these materials in a colorful, two-pocket folder. Don't enclose your originals; make photocopies of all materials. After all, the employer may be so impressed with your portfolio that he or she decides to keep it. Place one of your business cards in the portfolio (many two-pocket folders have die-cut slots designed to hold business cards) for a crisp, professional presentation.

Practice showing your portfolio. With a friend acting as a prospective employer, remove each item from the portfolio and explain its significance. Have your friend evaluate how well you showcased your materials and make any suggestions for improving your presentation.

COMPLETING EMPLOYMENT APPLICATIONS

Some employers may ask you to fill out an employment application before you are interviewed. You'll notice that the form asks for most of the information contained in your resumé. So why not just hand over your resumé and save all that writing? The application arranges the information for the employer's convenience.

To make the task of completing employment applications easier, bring a copy of your resumé with you. Follow the directions on the application carefully. Most will ask you to print or type the information. Do so neatly without spelling or grammar errors. For any section that doesn't apply to you, write N/A—which means Not Applicable—in the space. This tells the employer that you didn't skip over that section by mistake. You don't have to provide any information that is discriminatory, including your age, race, religion, marital status, and arrest record.

LAUNCHING YOUR JOB SEARCH

You've prepared your action plan—*My Job Search Plan*—organized your research and contacts in your job search notebook. As you move through the steps of your job search, take time periodically to carefully and objectively evaluate your progress. If you're not receiving offers, you may have to change your approach.

ATTAINING AND MAINTAINING A POSITIVE ATTITUDE

Attaining and maintaining a positive attitude throughout your job search may be your toughest task of all. One excellent strategy for stopping anxiety or depression from chipping away at your positive attitude is forming a job search team.

A job search team is a support group of other job seekers who are all looking for different jobs. Pull together five to ten job hunters and agree to meet every week. The meetings should be designed to encourage and support each other, to share job leads and job-hunting advice, and to exchange learning experiences and interviewing tips. Zip the lips when it comes to whining, carping, and complaining!

Have each person set goals for the week ahead—"I will mail resumés to ten companies this week," "I will spend an hour a day researching jobs on the Internet,"— and then report to the group at the next meeting on his or her accomplishments. After two weeks, ask each person to complete the following exercise.

FIVE POSITIVE RESULTS I'VE REALIZED FROM MY JOB SEARCH TEAM

■ *PURPOSE:* To evaluate the positive results of meeting with your job search team.

1. _____
   _____
   _____
   _____

2. _____
   _____
   _____
   _____

3. _____
   _____
   _____
   _____

4. _____
   _____
   _____
   _____

5. _____
   _____
   _____
   _____

If you can't find other job hunters in your area, a great place to meet and interact with other job seekers is the YAPA® member chat room. Go to www.yapa.com!

As you come to the end of this chapter, reflect on the next step of your journey of a thousand miles. You matched yourself to a career; set a career objective; learned the components of and how to conduct a successful, personalized job search; discovered how to create a resumé, cover letter, and portfolio; and picked up tips on attaining and maintaining a positive attitude.

You're on a roll, so don't quit now. Step into Chapter Three where you'll focus on success before, during, and after the interview. Come on, let's go!

Read All About It!

Anderson, Walter. *The Confidence Course: Seven Steps to Self-fulfillment.* New York, NY: Harper Perennial, 1998.

Boles, Richard Nelson. *What Color Is Your Parachute? A Practical Manual for Job Hunters and Career-Changers.* Berkeley, CA: Ten Speed Press, 1998.

Dimitrius, Jo-Ellan, Ph.D., & Mark Mazzarella. *Reading People: How to Understand People and Predict Their Behavior Any Time, Any Place.* New York, NY: Random House, 1998.

Josefowitz, Natasha. *Paths to Power: A Woman's Guide from First Job to Top Executive.* Reading, MA: Addison-Wesley Publishing Co., 1990.

Kaplan, Burton. *Winning People Over: 14 Days to Power and Confidence.* Upper Saddle River, NJ: Prentice Hall, 1996.

Moreau, Daniel. *Take Charge of Your Career: Survive and Profit from a Mid-Career Change.* Washington, DC: Kiplinger Books, 1996.

Richardson, Bradley G. *JobSmarts for Twentysomethings.* New York, NY: Vintage Books, 1995.

Rosenberg, Howard. *How to Succeed Without a Career Path: Jobs for People with No Corporate Ladder.* Manassas Park, VA: Impact Publications, 1995.

Scott, Steven K. *Simple Steps To Impossible Dreams: The Fifteen Power Secrets of the World's Most Successful People.* New York, NY: Simon & Schuster, 1998.

Tieger, Paul D., & Barbara Barron-Tieger. *The Art of Speed Reading People: Harness the Power of Personality Type and Create What You Want in Business and in Life.* New York, NY: Little Brown & Co., 1998.

Books I've Read

Use the space provided to list the books you've read in this subject area and to reflect on what you've learned from reading them.

1. _____
2. _____
3. _____
4. _____
5. _____

Internet Resources

http://www.selfgrowth.com

Self-Improvement Online, Inc. This Web site contains information on personal growth and provides links to other sites and newsgroups.

http://stats.bls.gov

U.S. Department of Labor's Bureau of Labor Statistics posts the *Occupational Outlook Handbook,* containing the latest job trend information.

http://www.ajb.dni/us/

America's Job Bank contains job listings posted by the public Employment Service and links to your state's employment office.

www.yapa.com

Young Adult Professional Associates, Inc.

My Favorite Internet Sites

Use the space provided to list your favorite Internet sites.

1. _____

2. _____

3. _____

4. _____

5. _____

SUCCESS Before, During, and After the Interview

Seeing things from the interviewer's angle as well as your own is at the heart of a successful job interview. But attaining a successful job interview begins even before you walk into the office of a prospective employer. You must research both the company and the job, know how to put your best foot forward during the interview, handle typical and tough questions, and know how to accept or decline a job offer based on whether or not the offer represents the right relationship. This chapter will help you to achieve success before, during, and after the interview.

After completing this chapter, you should understand:

- the various types of interviews you may face
- how to prepare for an interview
- what interviewers look for in a candidate
- how interviewers treat candidates
- how to shine during an interview
- what to do after an interview
- how to assess whether a job offer is right for you

> *If there is any one secret of success, it lies in the ability to get the other person's point of view and see things from his angle as well as from your own.*
>
> HENRY FORD,
> AMERICAN
> AUTOMOBILE PIONEER

If your cover letter and resume have done their job, you'll be contacted about scheduling an interview. The interview is the prospective employer's opportunity to evaluate your personal qualities, skills, and experience, but it is also your chance to learn as much as you can about the company and about the job. Since everything rides on how you behave before, during, and after the interview, preparation is vital. Making a good impression, asking intelligent questions, and showing your professionalism and interest are the success signposts along your journey of a thousand miles.

TYPES OF INTERVIEWS

What will your interview be like? Your interview may last only fifteen minutes or may stretch for an hour or longer. The interview might be conducted over the telephone with just you and the personnel manager, or the interview might take place as a conference call with you and a search committee. Telephone interviews save the employer time and money, especially if you are interviewing for a job located at a distance from where you live. However, most interviews are done in person. In-person interviews can be conducted one-on-one with the hiring manager or done with a search committee.

An in-person interview gives you a chance to see the actual work location and to meet some of the people you might be working with. Of course, having you on their turf gives the employer and your potential colleagues a chance to look you over as well. That thought combined with the importance of the interview will probably make you nervous. You know that this is your big chance to impress someone who can offer you a job, and you don't want to lose the opportunity. If you take the time before the interview to prepare and get psyched, chances are good that you will have a successful interview.

Preparing for the Interview

*P*art of your preparation for the interview is researching both the company and the job. Chapter Two contains strategies for doing initial research on the company. By contacting the company's public relations department, accessing business indexes at your library, or logging onto the company's Internet Web site, you should be able to access information about what the company sells or produces, if the company is small or large, if the company is for-profit or not-for-profit, what the company's reputation is in both the community and in the industry, and the kinds of problems the company might be facing. Review the form on which you captured this information—*My Prospective Employer Research*—which is stored in your job search notebook. With this basic information, you can now begin more in-depth research about the company.

1. *Obtain copies of the company's mission statement and annual reports.* When you are contacted about scheduling an interview, ask the person who calls to send you a copy of the company's mission statement and annual report for the current year and the previous year. If the current year's annual report isn't prepared yet, ask for the reports from the last two years. When you receive these materials, read them carefully, making notes about the company's significant achievements as well as their challenges. Then think about and make notes on what you can do for the company.

2. *Determine if you know anyone associated with the company.* Scan the list of senior staff or the members of the Board of Directors. Do any of the names ring a bell with you? Run the names by your job search team. Do any of the members know anyone associated with the company? Check with your family, your friends, your professors, and your school's placement

office to see if anyone has a link to anyone connected to the company.

If you are able to uncover a connection to someone within the company or on the Board, telephone that individual explaining that you have a job interview scheduled and that you're interested in learning more about the company. Most people you call will be glad to take ten minutes to give you an insider's view.

Try to focus the discussion around the challenges the company currently faces, remembering that opportunities are often disguised as problems. Ask also if your contact has any information about the job for which you will be interviewing or if the person knows of anyone inside the company who would be willing to speak with you about the job.

3. *Scan databases of local business periodicals.* Head to your local library's magazine and newspaper section and ask the librarian to point you in the direction of database indexes for local business periodicals. Do a search by company name for articles about the company that have appeared in the last six months. From the hits you get, read the full-text articles and add notes about the company to your job search notebook.

4. *Read current and back issues of the daily newspaper.* While you are in the periodicals section, ask the librarian for a cumulative index for the daily newspaper. Some indexes may be bound into books while others may be computer based. Do a keyword search by the name of the company and read a selection of articles about the company that have appeared within the last year. Make notes about your findings and add them to your job search notebook.

Once you've completed your in-depth research about the company, start researching information about the job itself. Chapter Two recommended that you check the

Occupational Outlook Handbook for a general description of your desired job. That's a good place to start, but keep in mind that job titles and descriptions may vary among different employers. You'll want to find out as much information as possible about the specific job for which you will be interviewing. Here's how to do that:

1. *Obtain a copy of the job description.* When you are called about scheduling an interview, ask the person from the company to send you a copy of the job description. Review the duties and responsibilities and assess how closely you come to being a match for the position. Note also if the job description contains a salary range.

2. *Check salary ranges for jobs. Occupational Outlook Handbook* and *National Survey of Professional, Administrative, Technical, and Clerical Pay* contain salary ranges for various jobs. Try to match the job title or job description to the listing in these library reference books to compare the salary range offered by the company to the typical salary range for that job.

3. *Speak with your company contact.* Your company contact may know something about the job and may be willing to share this information with you. But keep in mind that if your contact happens to be a member of the search committee charged with filling the position, he or she may feel that speaking to you about the job outside the context of an interview could be viewed as a conflict of interest. Respect this and withdraw your request, but ask if your contact can recommend anyone else that you could talk to.

4. *Check among the people in your network or on your job search team.* Find out if anyone you know is connected to someone working in a similar job. You might ask if someone in your network knows anyone who works or has worked for the company. Speaking with some-

one already working in a similar job or someone with present or past ties to the company can provide you with an invaluable insider's viewpoint.

After you've researched the company and the job, you should start to feel more comfortable because you've turned a huge unknown—who the company is and what the job requires—into solid information. You can now use that information to gain more self-confidence by role-playing the interview.

Role playing is, simply, acting. You pretend to be a job seeker, and a partner pretends to be a prospective employer. You both act out the performance of the interview, and then you and your partner evaluate your performance. Role playing gives you the chance to practice answering interview questions so you will be prepared when the real interview takes place. Think of role playing as the rehearsal that comes before the actual performance. Actors and actresses wouldn't dream of stepping out on a stage without having practiced their lines. Likewise, you shouldn't think of entering a real interview without having logged in some rehearsal time. You'll have a chance to practice role playing later in this chapter.

Another important factor to consider in preparing for your interview is your appearance. Chapter Two discussed creating a good first impression in the way you dress. You'll want to stick to the basics which is usually a clean, conservative, well-pressed suit. This applies to both men and women. Don't go to extremes with skimpy clothes, wild colors, large jewelry, massive body piercings, too much makeup, sunglasses, and sneakers. Avoid perfumes or aftershave.

Your appearance is determined not only by the clothing you choose but how you conduct yourself during the interview. Here are some suggestions for you to consider before the interview to make sure that your behavior shows your professionalism:

■ *Know the exact location of the interview and the best route to get there.* Arrive for the interview ten minutes early.

It looks bad if you are late, and you will be frazzled by the time you get there. If you get there early, you have the chance to visit the restroom to freshen up—comb your hair, pop in a breath mint, and straighten your clothing. If you feel nervous and if you're worried about offering the interviewer a cold, clammy handshake, here's a secret. Run your hands under hot water until your hands feel really warm. Dry them thoroughly with a paper towel and rub them hard. This will keep your hands warm and dry until you walk confidently into the office and offer your hand in greeting.

■ *Bring a copy of your portfolio plus two or three copies of your resume.* Make sure that the portfolio is a copy the interviewer may keep, not your original. If the interviewer has misplaced the resume you sent, you can provide a back-up copy. The interviewer may want you to meet other people in the company but may not think about or have time to make photocopies of your resume. That's a problem. Having extras with you will show that you are a problem solver.

■ *Pack a briefcase.* Include a pen, a small notebook, your list of references, a list of questions you have for the interviewer, and your planning calendar. You may be required to complete an employment application, and you may wish to make notes during the interview. The interviewer may ask for your list of references. If the interviewer wants you to return for a follow-up interview, you can set the date in your planning calendar.

■ *Avoid eating, chewing gum, or smoking* in the reception area or in the interview room.

■ *Be courteous to all you meet.* Smile, remember to say "please" and "thank you," and don't interrupt someone who is speaking.

■ *Make sure you know the interviewer's name.* Present your business card and ask for the interviewer's card. This way you'll know the person's name and you'll have the interviewer's title and the company's mailing address for the follow-up letter that you will send after the interview.

■ *During the interview, don't criticize or complain* about former employers, discuss your financial or personal problems, or get into arguments about controversial topics such as politics or religion.

■ *Be ready to take more than one test.* The interviewer may ask you to take a skills or aptitude test, a medical examination, or a drug test.

■ *Don't bring up the subject of salary and benefits.* You need to learn specifics about the job first before you can judge whether or not the salary and benefits are attractive. Your asking about money right off the bat gives the interviewer the impression that money is all you care about. The job that you can do is of paramount importance to the company, so you want to give the impression that the job is of paramount importance to you, too.

Think of it this way. Preparing for an interview is just the same as getting ready for a final exam. By being fully prepared, you will feel more comfortable and confident, and you'll ace any interview you go into.

Connie Davis

The Arc of the United States

"The resume has to do a good sales job for the applicant in order to be considered for an interview," according to Connie Davis, Director of Business Services for The Arc of the United States in Arlington, Texas. "I look for education, job longevity, job description matches, grammar, and spelling."

If the sales pitch is a good one, Davis invites candidates to interviews. She conducts a standard interview, discussing both the mission of the not-for-profit agency and the position.

"The one question I almost always ask is: 'I've told you about the requirements of the position, how do you feel your qualifications meet our needs?' The answer to this question tells me if the applicant has listened to the job description, how much job experience he or she has in this area, and what ideas he or she has in applying this experience or ability. It also helps me to determine the applicant's ability to think under pressure."

What makes a bad interview? "No eye contact," Davis says. "Also when a candidate talks around questions without answering them. If the question is asked, it deserves a direct answer"

For those preparing for interviews with her organization, Davis offers the following advice. "Learn something about the organization. If this is a first job, have someone help you by practicing. Be prepared to talk about your qualifications and work experience. Dress properly for the interview—conservative, not flashy. Be prompt."

> **In most cases, this [the resumé] is the first contact that an applicant has with the company.**

WHAT INTERVIEWERS LOOK FOR IN A CANDIDATE

An interviewer always represents the interests of the company, and the interviewer's challenge is to find the right person to fill a given position. You have your own interests in mind, and your challenge during the interview is to convince the interviewer that you are the right person for the position. In other words, you have to "sell" the idea that you are the best person for the job.

In the professional world, there is a lesson that takes the form of a question: What's everyone's favorite radio station? The answer is WII-FM, and the call letters stand for *What's In It For Me?* Many people have a WII-FM mentality. In order for you to "sell" the idea that you are the best person for the job, you have to set aside your own WII-FM—salary, benefits, perks—and focus on the WII-FM of the interviewer—what you can do for the company. So get the dollar signs out of your eyes and focus on projecting your desire to help the company solve problems. This is the first thing that interviewers look for in a candidate.

Interviewers also look for a candidate who is enthusiastic. Have an upbeat tone to your voice. Visualize yourself accepting the job offer and working at the company and let the excitement from that image be reflected in your speech, your body language, and your gestures.

Interviewers also look for a candidate who is committed to excellence, to team work, to professional growth and to development. If you can demonstrate examples from past jobs, your education, or your personal life that show that you share those same commitments, you will address "What's In It For Me" from the company's perspective, and it will add to the success of your job interview.

HOW INTERVIEWERS TREAT CANDIDATES

*M*ost interviewers want you to do your best, but how they treat you during the interview may not be designed with that in mind. Although many interviewers will be gracious, you may encounter others who are gruff, argumentative, and downright nasty. Is this an act? It could be! The interviewer may be testing you to see how you react under pressure and stress. Make sure you pass this test by being respectful and polite at all times. Don't lose your temper, even when provoked. Maintain your cool.

One way an interviewer may try to rattle you is by asking sensitive or personal questions. Questions relating to race, gender, age, religion, and marital status are discriminatory and sometimes illegal, but some interviewers ask them anyway. So what should you do?

Replying "That's none of your business" is the truthful answer, but it won't get you anywhere, and, in fact, may even antagonize the interviewer. Your best bet is to answer in a way that gets the interview back on track while sparing the interviewer any embarrassment (after all, some interviewers may not realize that some questions are inappropriate).

For example, the interviewer may ask your age. If you don't mind answering, tell how old you are, but keep in mind that you are not obligated to reply to such a question. If you're uncomfortable answering, phrase your reply this way: "The ad for this position didn't indicate a concern about age. I believe the ad focused on computer skills. I'd like to demonstrate my abilities with Word Perfect."

If your interview is filled with questions that seem to focus on inappropriate subject areas, the interviewer may be testing you, trying to make you lose your cool. Don't let this happen! Often the interviewer will praise you for maintaining control, and that will be your clue that it was all a test. On the other hand, if the interviewer persists in hammering you with questions that are discriminatory and doesn't let you know that it was a test, maybe it wasn't. That may indicate that you would be better off not working for that company.

How to Put Your Best Foot Forward in an Interview

*B*y being prepared, you'll be able to put your best foot forward during your interview. Use these suggestions to make sure that you shine:

1. *Use engaged posture and body language.* When you are invited into the interview room, introduce yourself to the interviewer, smile, and shake hands with a firm but not bone-crushing grip. This brief window of time will make or break the interview for you, according to psychologists.

   Researchers who have analyzed job interviews believe that most interviewers make up their minds about job candidates within the first thirty seconds of meeting them. This decision is based on what psychologists call the Halo Effect, meaning the effect meeting you for the first time has on the interviewer. If you trip on the carpet as you enter the office, the person meeting you for the first time will think you're clumsy. If you enter the office smiling and exuding self-confidence, the person meeting you for the first time will think you're self-assured, so make the most of the Halo Effect.

   Don't sit down until the interviewer invites you to take a seat and then directs you to a chair. Place your briefcase on the floor or on a chair next to you. Don't place any of your belongings on the interviewer's desk.

After you are asked to be seated, sit up straight and focus on the interviewer. Pretend that you want to make a friend of this person. Maintain eye contact, lean forward a little, and keep your arms open, not crossed. Your body language speaks louder than your words. If you lean back in your chair with arms crossed, you tell the interviewer that you either lack confidence or that you don't care about the job, the company, or the interviewer. Let your posture and body language shows that you are sincere, interested, and enthusiastic.

2. *Listen actively.* The Greek philosopher Zeno wrote that: "We have two ears and one mouth that we may listen the more and talk the less." Some people listen with only one ear. That means they take in only enough of the conversation to be able to smile and nod at the speaker and throw in an occasional "Uh-huh" to keep the speaker happy and the conversation rolling. That's passive listening. Active listening means that you listen with both ears: You concentrate on the speaker, you participate in the conversation, and your mind focuses on both.

    Techniques to help you listen actively include being physically prepared to hear. Sit close to the speaker so you can hear well, ask that doors and windows be closed to block out noise and distractions, and watch the speaker's nonverbal cues, which will help you interpret the message.

    After you are physically prepared to hear, you must be open to listening. That means you must be willing to receive the speaker's message in a non-judgmental way. This is hard because in most conversations, people tend to focus on the contradictions and errors of the message while the speaker is talking. Being open to listening requires you to accept willingly the speaker's right to say the message, to let the message enter your consciousness, and, once you've understood the message to evaluate it. Listening in this way communicates to the speaker that you believe he or she is important and that the speaker's ideas have value. In return, the speaker will be more open to you and will feel less defensive because he or she will know that you are not only listening but hearing what is being said.

Being an open listener also means you are curious about other people. If you can allow your curiosity to overcome your need to judge the speaker and to defend your own position, your efforts will be rewarded. You'll find that you'll learn much more than you thought you could.

Asking questions will satisfy your curiosity and allow you to clarify your understanding of the speaker's message. The best questions to ask are open-ended questions that begin with "What," "How," and "Why." Questions such as "What is the mission statement of the company?," "How does the company feel about professional development activities for new hires?," and "Why did the last person who held this job leave the position?" require the speaker to respond with an explanation and are designed to get more detail.

Close-ended questions—those that can be answered with "yes" or "no"—limit the exchange of information. But these questions can be helpful if you want to be clear about your understanding of the speaker's message. For example: "Did you say that the training period is six weeks long?"

3. *Answer questions concisely and honestly.* Some interviewers will ask you specific, targeted questions; others will say simply, "What can you tell me about yourself?" Think before you reply, ask for clarification of anything you don't understand about the question, and follow the interviewer's lead in answering. For specific, targeted questions, give a brief, to-the-point response. For open-ended questions, you can speak at length but try to be concise and avoid rambling or getting off the subject.

No matter what questions you are asked, answer them honestly. Don't give a reply you think the interviewer wants to hear and don't lie. If you do, you may find that your dishonesty comes back to haunt you later.

4. *Be ready to ask questions.* Your initial and in-depth research about the company and the job combined with the information you gain from your conversation with the interviewer should make it easy for you to think of questions to ask. As questions occur to you, jot them in your notebook and be sure you ask them at an appropriate moment.

   If the interviewer has covered all of your questions during the conversation, you may encounter that awkward moment when he or she asks you "What questions do you have?" You could mumble something like "Well, you've already covered everything," but interviewers expect you to ask questions. Don't panic! Interviewers plan their questions in advance, so there's no reason why you shouldn't have questions prepared ahead of time that you can ask during any interview. Here are some questions for you to consider. Write them on the last page of your small notebook, so you can turn to them immediately and avoid an uncomfortable silence:

   "What is this company like as a place to work?"

   "What can you tell me about the culture and company's values?"

   "What are the challenges your company is facing?"

   "Could you tell me about the primary people I would be working with?"

   "What career opportunities exist beyond the entry-level position?"

"What do you consider ideal experience for this job."

"The job sounds really exciting—what are the drawbacks?"

"How will my performance be measured?"

"What type of mentoring program does the company offer?"

"What are the opportunities for professional growth?"

"How do you see me helping you to meet the challenges you're facing?"

"How well do you think I'd fit into this job?"

Use the following exercise to create your own questions that you can ask during interviews.

■ **PURPOSE:** To develop questions to ask a prospective employer during an interview.

1. _____

_____

_____

_____

2. _____

_____

_____

_____

3. _____

_____

_____

_____

4. _____

_____

_____

_____

5. _____

_____

_____

_____

HANDLING TYPICAL AND TOUGH INTERVIEW QUESTIONS

*I*nterviewers have typical and sometimes tough questions they usually ask job candidates. How you handle the questions is vital.

Be certain to listen actively to the questions. You want to be sure to answer the question asked not the question you thought you heard. Answer a question with a question especially if you're not sure what information the interviewer is seeking.

If you've done your homework—you know yourself and what you want to achieve and you've researched both the company and the job—you'll be able to handle any question that's thrown at you. Here are some common interview questions, from typical to tough, and suggestions for ways you can handle them. Typical interview questions include:

1. *"What can you tell me about yourself?"* There's no right answer to this question, but since it's always asked you should have a plan for answering it so that your response puts you in the best light. You could start with highlights of your basic life history told in chronological order, spotlighting some of the past jobs you've held and strengths you bring to the workplace. Or you could paint an impressionistic portrait of yourself such as: "I'm someone who moves into new situations and gets things started. Everything I've done for the last five years..." Whichever way you choose, make certain that you include a description of your skills— "I write quickly and easily,"—and link each skill to an example from your work experience. Make sure that your answer is brief and concise. The interviewer isn't interested in a forty-minute monologue.

2. *"Why do you want to work for us?"* From the research you've conducted about the company, pick two or

three good reasons for wanting to work there. For example, maybe your research has uncovered that the company plans to open a new branch office. You might mention that and add, "I'm very much interested in being part of a company that's expanding."

3. *"Where would you like to be five years from now?"* You know the answer to this because it's part of your long-term career strategy. If you can compare your goals with the growth possibilities of the prospective company, you'll breeze through this question. But avoid telling the interviewer that you'll be doing his or her job five years from now. That may be an honest response, but it'll be perceived as a threat. Instead say something like: "I'd like to work with you, helping to grow this company."

4. *"What do you like best about your work?"* Emphasize the elements you know will be part of the position. For example, if you know you'll be part of a work team say: "I enjoy the challenge of working and solving problems with a group of dedicated individuals."

5. *"What was your most difficult or complex project that was challenging to you."* This question tries to get at various managerial skills such as planning and organizing, interpersonal effectiveness, communication effectiveness, etc. Be prepared to answer the question by explaining how you handled a project by setting priorities, resolving conflicts, overcoming obstacles. Use your experiences from previous work, school, extracurricular, community volunteer, military, or personal experiences.

Other typical interview questions include:

"Why did you enter your job field?"

"What is the ideal job for you?"

"Why did you pick your major?"

"What courses did you like best/least and why?"

"Have you had any special training for this job?"

"What would you do to improve our company?"

"Could I see samples of your work?"

"What are your three greatest strengths?"

"What are your greatest accomplishments so far?"

"What are some of your outside interests and activities?"

Tough interview questions can include questions similar to the ones that follow:

1. *"Why do you want to leave your current position?"* Approach this potential mine field carefully. If you answer negatively—"My boss is a jerk," the interviewer could think that you'd feel the same way about the boss at the new company, and if the interviewer is the boss-to-be, you've just sunk your chances of getting hired. Instead, answer the question positively, keeping in mind WII-FM: "I enjoy my present position, but it's time for me to grow. I also see this position as a way of using my background to help your company move ahead."

2. *"What are you looking for?"* Job seekers often think that this question refers to salary, benefits, and perks, and if you respond that way, you've lost an opportunity to show how hiring you would be mutually beneficial. Instead, say something like: "I'm looking for a chance to realize my full potential through a real challenge," or "I enjoy being part of a problem-solving team that helps the company grow."

3. *"What is your greatest weakness?"* Watch out for this one! This is not the moment for true confessions such as "I can't meet deadlines," or "I'm completely disorganized," or "Details bore me." The trick to answering this question is to come up with a weakness

and turn it into an strength. For example, many people consider it a weakness to be a perfectionist, especially if the perfectionist is unable to meet deadlines. So if you view yourself this way, turn this weakness into a strength: "I'm a perfectionist. I like taking a project and working on it until I get the job done right, and I always meet my deadlines."

4. *"Why have you changed jobs so frequently?"* Variations of this question include "Why are you unemployed?" and "Why have you been unemployed?" Be honest by giving the reasons for frequent job changes or for unemployment—focusing on positive rather than negative reasons. For example: "I regretted leaving my last position because the company was great to work for. Unfortunately, my hours were changed, which made it impossible for me to attend school. My boss and I agreed that completing my degree was more important."

5. *"Why should I hire you?"* Since you know the requirements of the job, parallel the needs of the company to your top skills and qualifications. Cover the top three needs of the company and show how your background and experience make you perfect for the job.

6. *"What salary are you expecting?"* Tactfully avoid answering this question early in the interview by saying something like: "While salary is an important issue, at this point I'm interested in learning more about how I would fit into this position." Then ask a question that will get the interview back on less volatile ground. By talking salary before you know about the job's responsibilities and the range of salary the company is offering, the salary figure you state may be too low or too high.

Use the following exercise to draft answers to three typical and three tough interview questions. Rehearse your answers before you go on an interview.

■ *PURPOSE:* To develop answers to typical questions that are asked during an interview.

Question # 1: "What can you tell me about yourself?"

My Answer: _____

_____

_____

_____

_____

Question #2: "Why do you want to work for us?"

My Answer: _____

_____

_____

_____

_____

Question #3: "Where would you like to be five years from now?"

My Answer: _____

_____

_____

_____

_____

■ **PURPOSE:** To develop answers to tough questions that are asked during an interview.

Question # 1: "What are you looking for?"

My Answer: _____

_____

_____

_____

_____

Question #2: "What is your greatest weakness?"

My Answer: _____

_____

_____

_____

_____

Question #3: "Why should I hire you?"

My Answer: _____

_____

_____

_____

_____

After all the typical and tough questions have been asked, the interviewer will close the interview. This can happen in one of three ways.

■ *The interviewer might thank you for your time* and tell you that you'll hear from the company after all interviews have been conducted. You can ask when you might expect to hear and make a note of this in your notebook.

■ *The interviewer might ask you to return for a second interview* or for an aptitude or medical test. Ask for details about any test you are asked to take. If you are invited back, jot the details of the appointment in your notebook.

■ *The interviewer might offer you the job.* If this happens, ask for a day or two to consider the offer, even if you know you really want the job. This gives you time to talk to other people and to think about whether the company, job, salary, and potential for growth mesh with your career objective and your long-term goals.

THE ALL-IMPORTANT FOLLOW-UP LETTER

No matter how the interview ends, you should send a brief letter to the interviewer, thanking him or her for taking the time to meet with you. Your letter will reinforce the points you made during the interview and will show your level of interest in the company and the job. Use the following samples to guide you in the writing of your follow-up letters.

Jesse Three Crows

23 First Street ■ Albany, NY 12208

(518) 555-3647 ■ jthreecrows@aol.com

February 15, 1999

Ms. Amee Wong
Human Resources Manager
Cutler & Quigley, Inc.
35 South Hills Road
Clifton Park, NY 12065

Dear Ms. Wong:

Thank you for taking the time to meet with me yesterday about the assistant accountant position at Cutler & Quigley, Inc. I believe my experience in bookkeeping, payroll services, tax preparation, and computer and interpersonal skills would contribute to the success of the position we discussed.

I was impressed with your company, and I believe I would be a valuable addition to your staff. I would appreciate your serious consideration of my candidacy for the assistant accountant position.

Thank you again for the opportunity to meet with you and to learn about your company. I look forward to hearing from you.

Sincerely,

Jesse Three Crows

Jesse Three Crows

23 First Street ■ Albany, NY 12208

(518) 555-3647 ■ jthreecrows@aol.com

February 15, 1999

Ms. Amee Wong
Human Resources Manager
Cutler & Quigley, Inc.
35 South Hills Road
Clifton Park, NY 12065

Dear Ms. Wong:

Thank you for taking the time to meet with me yesterday about the assistant accountant position at Cutler & Quigley, Inc.

Although we agreed that my qualifications are not in line with your needs at this time, I wanted to let you know how tremendously impressed I was by the quality of work being done at your company. Therefore, I hope you will keep me in mind should a more suitable opening occur.

If you learn of other companies in need of talents like mine, I would greatly appreciate your bringing my resume to their attention.

Thank you again for the opportunity to meet with you and to learn about Cutler & Quigley, Inc. I hope we will have the opportunity to meet again.

Sincerely,

Jesse Three Crows

Now that you have a good overview of the interview process, use the role-playing exercise that follows to become comfortable and confident in an interview situation.

INTERVIEW ROLE-PLAYING

■ *PURPOSE:* To become comfortable and confident in an interview situation.

1. Choose a friend who is willing to play the part of the interviewer. Ask your friend to develop a list of interview questions to ask you.

_____

_____

_____

2. Prepare a list of responses to typical and tough interview questions.

_____

_____

_____

3. Enact a mock interview session.

_____

_____

_____

4. After the session, discuss how well you think you did during the interview. Ask your friend to evaluate your performance. What did you do well during the interview? What did you do that you could do better?

_____

_____

_____

_____

_____

SECOND INTERVIEWS

*I*f you made a strong impression in the initial interview, you may be called back for a second interview. Second interviews are often opportunities for managers in the company or the team members you'll work with to meet you. Treat second interviews just as you do first interviews and follow the same recommendations for giving a spectacular presentation. Don't get overconfident. Just because you've been called back doesn't mean you have the inside track to the job. The company may be calling back other candidates, too.

Second interviews can be less nerve wracking because you're familiar with the company and the person who initially interviewed you. But if you have to face a number of individuals or an entire search committee, you're knees will be knocking before you know it. Take a few deep breaths and visualize a successful encounter before you go in.

The questions you will be asked during a second interview tend to be focused more on the skills and abilities you can bring to the company. Be prepared by bringing copies of your portfolio and real-life examples from work or school with you. These will help to demonstrate how you've used your skills and abilities to accomplish what you've achieved in various areas. Strive to match your qualifications to the needs of the company and the specific requirements of the job.

Follow up a second interview with a note to the person who arranged the interview. Thank the person for his or her time and interest in you and mention your excitement at the possibility of joining the company. Then, cross your fingers and hope that the search committee selects you for the position.

WHEN YOU ARE NOT SELECTED FOR A JOB

*U*nfortunately, you won't receive a job offer for every interview you go on. But you can use every interview as a stepping stone to the next one. Review your performance and make notes in your job search notebook. Use the following exercise to evaluate yourself.

MY INTERVIEW EVALUATION

■ *PURPOSE:* To evaluate your performance during an interview.

1. The interviewer seemed most impressed by:

_____

_____

2. The interviewer seemed least impressed by:

_____

_____

3. I did the following things well:

_____

_____

4. The following things I did need improvement:

_____

_____

5. I can make improvements by:

_____

_____

WHEN YOU ARE OFFERED A JOB

*H*ooray! The phone call from the company came, and the human resource manager offered you the job. You're thrilled! But don't accept just yet because some issues still must be worked out.

The human resource manager will invite you to the company to discuss the aspects of the offer, including compensation, benefits, and details about the job itself. Use the following checklist to make sure that all areas are covered and add any questions that pertain to your special circumstances.

JOB OFFER CHECKLIST

1. The salary is: _____

2. Does the company pay for overtime?   ❏ Yes   ❏ No

3. What is the pay schedule?   ❏ Weekly   ❏ Biweekly   ❏ Monthly

4. Does the company offer a pension or investment plan?   ❏ Yes   ❏ No

5. Can I contribute to the pension or investment plan?   ❏ Yes   ❏ No

6. Does the company match my contributions?   ❏ Yes   ❏ No

7. The percentage matched by the company is: _____

8. When do I earn vested rights in the plan? _____

9. Does the company provide tuition reimbursement?   ❏ Yes   ❏ No

10. The company's vacation policy is: _____

11. The company's holiday/sick leave policy is: _____

12. The company offers these insurance benefits: _____

13. The company dress code is: _____

14. The standard work schedule is: _____

15. Is flex-time an option?   ❏ Yes   ❏ No

16. I am expected to begin work on: _____

17. The work I will be doing includes: _____

_____

18. Other areas of concern for me include: _____

_____

ASSESSING A JOB OFFER

*O*nce the company has made its offer, you owe it to yourself to review it. The offer is the beginning of a business relationship, and you need to decide if this is the right relationship for you. Consider the following:

1. *Is the job a good match for you?* Probably the most important factor is your fit within the organization. Did you enjoy meeting the people who worked at the company? If you met your immediate supervisor, do you think that he or she is a person you'll feel comfortable working for? What was the climate of the company? Rigid or open? Decide whether there is an appropriate level of challenge to the position. Will you have the opportunity to participate in the kinds of activities you're interested in? Will the job provide the growth you'll need to meet your eventual career goals?

2. *Will you have a mentor?* Look for a job in which there will be someone who will take a personal interest in your professional career; someone who will give you the opportunity to try new or different things; someone who is supportive but candid with you.

3. *Are there opportunities for advancement?* No one wants to get stuck in a dead-end job. Look back in your notebook for the interviewer's answer to this question: "What career opportunities exist beyond the entry-level position?" The answer will give you information about the career path that leads out of the position you're considering. Does the job seem to hold promise for positions you would like to have?

4. *What are the fringe benefits?* Some desirable fringes include: employer-paid health and dental insurance, tuition reimbursement, pension or profit-sharing plan,

company car, free parking, relevant seminars and sym-
posiums, professional memberships, relocation assistance, and interim living expenses. What is important
to you?

5. *Is the salary in line with your skills and experience?* Your
   library research has uncovered salary ranges for similar positions, but how does your own market value
   impact on that range?

   Ask the human resource manager for a day or two to
consider the offer. Then use the following exercise to
determine what you want from a company.

MY COMPANY WISH LIST

■ **PURPOSE:** To determine the factors important to you for accepting a job.

List ten things that are important for you to have from a prospective employer. Your list could include a specific level of salary, challenging work environment, tuition reimbursement, etc.

1. _____
   _____

2. _____
   _____

3. _____
   _____

4. _____
   _____

5. _____
   _____

6. _____
   _____

7. _____
   _____

8. _____
   _____

9. _____
   _____

10. _____
    _____

Next, rank your list of ten things in priority order, assigning #1 to the thing that is most important to you and #10 to the thing that is least important to you.

1. _____

_____

2. _____

_____

3. _____

_____

4. _____

_____

5. _____

_____

6. _____

_____

7. _____

_____

8. _____

_____

9. _____

_____

10. _____

_____

(Continued)

Last, compare your prioritized list of things with the offer made by the company.

	My List	Their Offer
1.		
2.		
3.		
4.		
5.		
6.		
7.		
8.		
9.		
10.		

From these answers, you will be able to determine if this offer represents the right relationship for you.

THE ART OF NEGOTIATING: SALARY, BENEFITS, PERKS

*E*ven when you determine that the offer represents the right relationship, you shouldn't bite at the first package dangled in front of you. The name of the game is negotiating, and since the company definitely wants you, you have the power to get more of what you need.

If you know the range of salaries for the job in your industry and in your part of the country, you can judge how close the company's offer is to the minimum you were expecting. If you were expecting a higher level, you could respond by indicating a range you would consider. For example: "I believe that a salary range of between _____ and _____ fits both my experience and this job. I believe this because (cite your reasons). Don't you agree?"

If the human resource manager agrees, you're golden. If not, you need to negotiate for a salary that you can both be comfortable with. Don't be greedy but do be sure you accept a salary that is in line with your skills and abilities.

Benefits and perks can sometimes be negotiated at some companies. At others, the benefits package is fixed and non-negotiable. Ask the personnel director about the company's policy toward benefits.

If benefits and perks are negotiable, you need to look at the package and determine what you want or need in terms of fringes and perks. If the offer includes no vacation during the first year and two weeks in the second, you might negotiate for two weeks during the first year and three weeks thereafter. If the offer includes partial tuition reimbursement for any course you take, you might negotiate for total reimbursement for any course you take that is directly related to your job. Enter negotiations with the spirit of win/win, and you'll reach a compromise that works for both you and the company.

DECLINING A JOB OFFER

*S*ometimes the company doesn't have the flexibility to offer you more than is already on the table with the initial offer. Then you must decide if you should accept the offer just to have a job or if it would be better for you to continue job hunting. If you decide to continue job hunting, you must decline the offer. Do so promptly and professionally by telephoning the human resource manager and then by sending a follow-up letter, thanking the company for the offer and expressing your regret that you were unable to accept the position. Don't burn any bridges and leave the door open for future job possibilities.

ACCEPTING A JOB OFFER

*O*nce you have a final, attractive offer on the table, you'll be eager to accept the job. Let the personnel director know as soon as you have decided. The company may ask you to sign a letter of agreement that spells out the terms of employment. Review this letter carefully to make sure the terms represent accurately the items you negotiated.

The letter of agreement will also indicate the date and time you are to report for work. Circle that date on your planning calendar, sign the letter of agreement and pop it in the mail, then take some time to celebrate. You've landed a job, and you've taken a giant step on the path of your journey of a thousand miles.

Accepting an offer is only the beginning of your career. Step into Chapter Four where you'll focus on the next step of your journey of a thousand miles—finding success through networking.

Read All About It!

Ball, Frederick W., & Barbara B. Ball. *Killer Interviews*. New York, NY: McGraw-Hill, 1996.

Beatty, Richard H. *175 High-Impact Resumes*. New York, NY: John Wiley & Sons, 1996.

Besson, Taunee. *Cover Letters: Proven Techniques for Writing Letters That Will Help You Get the Job You Want*. New York, NY: John Wiley & Sons, 1995.

Betrus, Michael, & Jay A. Block. *101 Best Resumes*. New York, NY: McGraw-Hill, 1997.

Eyler, David R. *Job Interviews That Mean Business*. New York, NY: Random House, 1996.

Falke, Martha. *The First Four Seconds: Things Successful Men Know About Dressing for Power*. San Antonio, TX: Falcon House, 1991.

Farr, J. Michael, Sara Hall, & Susan Christophersen. *Why Should I Hire You: How To Do Well in Job Interviews*. Indianapolis, IN: Jist Works, 1992.

Kennedy, Joyce Lain. *Job Interviews for Dummies*. Chicago, IL: IDG Books Worldwide.

Koren, Leonard, & Peter Goodman. *The Haggler's Handbook: One Hour To Negotiating Power*. New York, NY: W.W. Norton & Company, 1991.

Krannich, Caryl, & Ronald L. Krannich. *Interview for Success: A Practical Guide to Increasing Job Interviews, Offers, and Salaries*. 7th ed. Manassas Park, VA: Impact Publications, 1998.

Lavington, Camille, with Stephanie Losee. *You've Only Got Three Seconds: How to Make the Right Impression in Your Business and Social Life*. New York, NY: Doubleday, 1997.

McDonnell, Sharon. *You're Hired!: Secrets to Successful Job Interviews*. New York, NY: Macmillan General Reference.

Marler, Patty, Jan Bailey Mattia, and Sarah Kennedy. *Job Interviews Made Easy*. Lincolnwood, IL: VGM Career Horizons, 1995.

Morgan, Dana. *10 Minute Guide to Job Interviews*. New York, NY: Arco, 1998.

O'Malley, Michael. *Are You Paid What You're Worth?* New York, NY: Broadway Books, 1998.

Yeager, Neil, and Lee Hough. *Power Interviews: Job-Winning Tactics from Fortune 500 Recruiters*. New York, NY: John Wiley & Sons, 1990.

Books I've Read

Use the space provided to list the books you've read in this subject area and to reflect on what you've learned from reading them.

1. _____
2. _____
3. _____
4. _____
5. _____

Internet Resources

http://www.collegeboard.org
The College Board has a career questionnaire on its Web site. Answer the questions and match yourself by ability, skills, and temperament to specific careers.

http://www.review.com/career
The Princeton Review site has a similar questionnaire and also contains job-hunting suggestions.

My Favorite Internet Sites

Use the space provided to list your favorite Internet sites.

1. _____
2. _____
3. _____
4. _____
5. _____

SUCCESS Through Networking

People who have dreams are people who are going somewhere. "Somewhere" isn't a vague location because these people know exactly where they're headed. You can be among them, and they can help you along the way. That's what networking is all about. The golden rule of networking is: Do more for others than they do for you. This chapter will help you to accomplish this.

After completing this chapter, you should understand:

- the definition of formal and informal networking

- the win/win aspects of networking

- how to be open to networking opportunities

- how to promote yourself through taking action and getting involved

- how to appreciate those who make your success a little easier

> ❝**D**o not surround yourself with people who do not have dreams.❞
>
> NIKKI GIOVANNI,
> AMERICAN POET

In the computer world, a network links many separate PCs for optimal operation of an enterprise. In the business world, a network links many separate people for optimal performance in finding a job, forging a career, and focusing on life-long success.

WHAT IS NETWORKING?

Networking is the process of making, using, and retaining both professional and personal relationships with the goal of exchanging information or services among individuals, groups, or institutions. Through networking, you develop personal resources as a result of your ability to pay attention, take action, become involved, and show your appreciation for the positive gestures and actions of others.

Think of every encounter you have with another person as a form of networking. Be on your best behavior, be confident, be prepared to speak about your goals, and be willing to listen for ways you can assist other people in the achievement of their goals. You will find amazing benefits if you consistently practice networking strategies throughout the developmental stages of your career and beyond.

INFORMAL VERSUS FORMAL NETWORKING

Networking can be informal or formal. Formal networking takes place during informational interviews, when cold calling prospective employers, at career fairs, through internships, and while job shadowing. You can also find opportunities for formal networking at meetings of professionals in your field, at business-to-business exchange events sponsored by a local Chamber of Commerce, and during gatherings of your church or temple.

Informal networking can take place anywhere with anybody—your family and friends, those you know at school and at work, individuals with whom you share recreational or sporting activities, people you meet on-line, the butcher, the banker, the candlestick maker.

For example: Alexis E. is a writer with a long-term career objective of becoming a screenplay writer for Hollywood. She enhances her writing skills by taking credit-free courses in creative writing, nonfiction writing, and juvenile fiction writing at a local community college. Recently, Alexis signed up for a course in writing and publishing books.

"I thought it would be fun to learn about book publishing in case I want to turn one of my screenplays into a novel," Alexis said. On the first night of class, the instructor asked the students to introduce themselves and to tell why they had enrolled in the course.

"I gave my little spiel," Alexis said, "and included the fact that my ultimate goal was screenplay writing and that I was looking for an agent. I knew it didn't fit with the scope of the course, but I threw it in anyway. As it turned out, one of the other students was originally from Los Angeles, where she had worked for an agent who handles screenplays. She gave me his name and number and said that I could mention that she had referred me. I contacted him, he remembered her, and he agreed to read one of my scripts. It's not easy to get an agent, and I wouldn't have been able to make that connection on my own."

Jose R. works part-time in the shipping department of a large department store while finishing his four-year business degree. His career objective is to break into retail sales. At the store's staff holiday party, Jose introduced himself to the manager of the men's wear department and spent some time discussing industry issues and the particular challenges of running a specialty department. "We had a terrific conversation, and I told him about my wanting to start a career in sales," Jose said. "A few weeks later I found a journal article at school that had some good ideas for handling one of the problems he and I had discussed at the party. I made a copy of the article and some notes about how a few of the ideas could be implemented at the store. Then I dropped it off at his office."

The manager appreciated Jose's initiative and ideas. He called Jose to thank him and to mention that when the next sales associate opening occurred he would let Jose know.

"I felt great because my wanting to help him made him willing to help me," Jose said.

THE WIN/WIN ASPECTS OF NETWORKING

Jose's comments point out the win/win aspects of networking. According to Stephen R. Covey in his best-selling book *The 7 Habits of Highly Effective People*, "Win/win is a frame of mind and heart that constantly seeks mutual benefit in all human interactions...Win/win is based on the paradigm that there is plenty for everybody, that one person's success is not achieved at the expense or exclusion of the success of others."

Networking based solely on self-centered wants tends to be a lose/lose proposition. If your sole purpose in networking rests upon your own desires, you will soon be exposed and shunned by people.

People don't want to be, nor do they deserve to be, used. The benefits of networking and paying attention to the people and situations around you is to learn from what you're doing, to see the benefits and the win/win situations that can come if networking is conducted correctly.

Networking is conducted correctly when the golden rule of networking is applied: Do more for others than they do for you. It really is that simple. Over time, you will derive from networking only what you put into it. So, if you want someone to help you, help him or her first. That's when you get to win/win.

Michelle Buenau-Ciccone

AT&T

Once you've accepted a position and started your job, you have a perfect opportunity to get to know people in the company and to begin building relationships by using your free time wisely. Michelle Buenau-Ciccone, Human Assets Leader at AT&T in Albany, New York, suggests that you go to lunch with people from different levels in the company from secretaries and receptionists to managers and vice presidents. "These individuals can get you involved in extracurricular activities in the office," Ciccone said. "When you get involved in golf tournaments, softball games, or community events, you get to meet people from various levels, and those relationships are important."

In addition to becoming involved, Ciccone also suggests taking a leadership role in the activities you join. "It will show that you're being proactive," Ciccone said. "Don't just sit back and wait for people to come to you. Take five minutes everyday and ask yourself, 'What are the pro-active things that I can do that are not part of my job that will help me to be more successful?'

Your involvement in activities may require that you work extra hours each week, but Ciccone believes that the investment of those hours will contribute to your success. "First impressions count," she said. "If you start out doing a great job, both in your work and in your extra-work activities, you'll become known as someone who's a go-getter, someone who takes the initiative. You'll get recognition, and you'll meet people, not just in your field but in other industries as well."

For Ciccone, success is built one relationship at a time. What can you do today to begin building relationships that will add to your success?

> *Try to get involved in those things [outside activities] because you're going to meet people, not just in your field but in other industries as well.*

*H*ow do you network with people you don't even know? This is a common question best answered by relating business networking to a form of social networking you've probably experienced—dating.

Imagine that someone you'd like to meet and get to know catches your eye. You see this person every day, but the individual seems oblivious to you. What can you do to make a connection? You might begin by finding out something about the person—name, where the person lives or goes to school, other places the person frequents. You might determine if you have a mutual friend or acquaintance. You tap into any and all outside resources that will bring the two of you together in a social, academic, or work-related setting. As crazy as it may sound, this is networking.

Simple in theory, isn't it? In practice, networking isn't that difficult either. Networking is a skill learned as any skill would be, and the practice of networking starts by making a connection.

Networking is really only a series of connections that form a network of people working toward the same goal. When all the connections are made, the network is up and running. Picture a million people networking with each other. What do you think that can do for you and for them? Plenty.

The more people who know and respect you based on your professional conduct, the better your chances for successful networking. Successful networking results when you know yourself—your goals, your strengths, and your weaknesses—and when you remain open for opportunities, when you see the potential for a relationship that might not be obvious on the surface.

For example, perhaps you meet a computer programmer at a social engagement. If you aren't interested in computer programming, you might make the mistake of thinking that investing time in getting to know this person might not be of much value. But if you take the time to understand what this person does, who the individual works for, where the person went to school, you will probably discover information that might be useful in the future. Maybe the person works for a company that interests you. Perhaps the person has friends working for companies in which you are trying to gain access. Maybe the person knows the hard-to-reach human resource manager at one of your prime company targets.

Be an opportunist. Look beneath the surface and do some conversational probing in a nice and friendly manner. At a minimum, you'll get to know someone better. Quite possibly that brief conversation could lead you right through the door of your next employer.

Be an exchanger of business cards. Keep plenty of your own handy and offer one at the end of a conversation. Most likely the person will reciprocate.

Keep all the cards you acquire. In fact, consider getting a business card portfolio which is a vinyl folder containing slots for the safe keeping of the cards you collect. Before you store each card, jot a note on the back that will refresh your memory about the person. For example, you might indicate the event at which you met the person, the name of a friend you have in common, or a special interest the person mentioned. The business card becomes an immediate and invaluable source for follow-up that helps you build the relationship.

PROMOTING YOURSELF

Part of relationship building is practicing follow-up and at the same time promoting yourself. After meeting someone, send a letter indicating how pleased you were to have met and how much you enjoyed the conversation. Drop a business card into the envelope. Receiving a letter and card may prompt the person to call you with a job lead or an invitation for lunch.

If not, you can be proactive. Review your collection of business cards and the notes you made on the back, looking for follow-up opportunities. For example, maybe someone you spoke to admired your briefcase and asked for information on where to get one like it. Pick up the phone and say: "Hello, this is _____. We met at the Chamber's business mixer last week, and you were interested in a briefcase like mine as a gift for your brother. I dug into my files and found that I bought it at Cedar's Luggage Shop in the downtown mall last year. The style number is 763545. I hope that helps you."

Thoughtfulness such as this will make the person remember you positively, and you never know how this will benefit you in the long run.

As the months roll by, you can nurture relationships by keeping in touch with people you've met. Make quick phone calls to share good news or, if you've had a particularly difficult time, call to ask advice. Your willingness to share your victories as well as your concerns causes people to be involved in your career and feel a vested interest in your future success.

PAYING ATTENTION

Just as you expect people to listen to you, you should be prepared to listen and to pay attention to those who contribute to your life.

When making new acquaintances, one of the biggest mistakes people make is not remembering names. You've probably had the experience of walking into a room, meeting someone and shaking hands, hearing the person's name, and then, seconds later, you realize you've forgotten the name you just heard. You wrack your brain trying to remember, then admit defeat and feel forced to say:

"I'm sorry. Would tell me your name again?" Talk about embarrassing.

Remembering names is an important part of the initial stages of networking and shows that you are paying attention and are interested in the individual you've just met. If you can walk into a room, meet ten people and leave hours later, saying good-bye to each person using his or her name, people will be astonished. Plus, they will remember you.

To avoid the embarrassment of forgetting someone's name, try these strategies.

1. *Memory Strategy #1.* Upon meeting someone, make a point to say his or her name aloud at least three times during the conversation. The best time to do this is when asking a question. For example: "Where do you work, Lorraine?" This will allow the person's name to be deposited in your memory banks.

2. *Memory Strategy #2.* When you meet someone, focus on something distinctive about the person. Is he wearing a flowered yellow tie? Does she have a red bow in her hair? Does she have bright blue eyes? Are his hands large? The first thing you notice about a person can be anything at all: something temporary such as clothing or jewelry the person is wearing or something permanent such as a striking physical feature, gestures, or body language. Then you need to associate the distinctive feature with the person's name. For example: Miss Red Bow = Mary.

3. *Memory Strategy # 3.* Upon meeting someone, break down the person's name into syllables then think about the sound of each syllable. What images do the syllables trigger for you? For a simple name such as Bill, you might think of the image of a dollar bill. Or the name Mike might make you think of the image of a microphone. For longer names, think of multiple images. For example, the name Nicole may make you think of the image of a nickel or the image of a nick on

a piece of coal. The name Wallace may make you think of the image of a walrus or the image of a wall with lace on it. Turn the name into the image, and you'll burn the name into your memory.

4. *Memory Strategy #4.* This strategy builds on the three previous ones. When you meet a person, say his or her name at least three times during the conversation. Focus on a distinctive feature and associate that feature with the person's name. The previous example was: Miss Red Bow = Mary. Then think about the sounds of the syllables in the person's name. Ask yourself what the sounds make you think of. For example, the name Mary might make you think of Merry as in Merry Christmas. Then think of an action that combines the distinctive feature and the image created by the sound of the person's name. You might think of tying red bows all over a merry Christmas tree. When you see that person again, even if she isn't wearing her distinctive bow, the image that will pop into your mind will be one of tying red bows all over a merry Christmas tree, and you'll remember her name: Mary.

By remembering names, you've achieved the first step in networking. A common trait among people is that they like to hear the sound of the their own name. This gives them a comfortable feeling and makes them feel friendly toward the person speaking the name. They will warm up to you and tell you a bit about themselves, and this is the start of building that business or social relationship, and all because you took the time to pay attention.

Taking Action

*I*f you're going to sell a product, it seems only logical that you would want to know as much about the product as you can. While networking, you are the product, and although you might think that you know who you are and what you want to achieve, it's important to stay in tune with yourself at all times.

Practicing personal growth and improvement by knowing yourself is just as important as eating well, getting enough rest, and exercising regularly. Know your priorities and goals and review them every day.

If you don't make a concerted effort to stay focused on your priorities and goals, you'll have difficulty remembering them when you need them the most: when you have a chance meeting with the human resources director or one of the administrators of the company you're going after. You could easily lose an important contact or networking opportunity because you were caught up in an otherwise insignificant conversation and didn't notice points of the conversation that would have provided you with a chance to sell yourself.

For every person you meet, conduct a mental discovery process to find out as much as you can about each person: where the person works, for whom the person works, what the person does, the associations the person belongs to, who his or her friends are, etc. Then think of your priorities and goals and begin to make connections that can prove to be mutually beneficial.

Another strategy for taking action is to play a game called Benefactor Bingo. The game is fun, but it's also serious because winning the game will help you advance toward your goals. Here's how it works.

■ **PURPOSE:** To keep track of your various goals.

Compile a list of sixteen traits, experiences, or pieces of information that you would like to gain over the next year. These could include developing into a great listener, meeting a newspaper executive, or understanding desk-top publishing.

1. _____
2. _____
3. _____
4. _____
5. _____
6. _____
7. _____
8. _____
9. _____
10. _____
11. _____
12. _____
13. _____
14. _____
15. _____
16. _____

Create a Benefactor Bingo Card (see the following sample) using each of sixteen traits, experiences, or pieces of information in a four-across and four-down arrangement. An aspiring commercial artist might have a Benefactor Bingo Card like the following.

Find a Mentor in the Ad Business	Investment Advisor	Experienced Graphic Artist	Guest Speaker
Project Manager	Great Listener	Small Business Owner	Travel Agent
Ad Agency Executive	Newspaper Executive	Magazine Employee	Billboard Co. Employee
Book Publisher	Venture Capitalist	Young Attorney	Commercial Artist

Review your Benefactor Bingo Card prior to attending any business or social function. Each time you meet someone who can help you meet the objective of one of the squares, place an "X" in the square. Each time you achieve BINGO (four in a row) reward yourself by doing something you enjoy.

Benefactor Bingo allows you to use to your advantage the serendipity of chance networking encounters. The next exercise asks you to plan proactively the encounters that will move you closer to your goals.

■ **PURPOSE:** To plan networking encounters.

Review the list you compiled for Benefactor Bingo—sixteen traits, experiences, or pieces of information that you would like to gain over the next year. For each item on your list, write the name and affiliation of any person you can think of who can provide the information you need. (It's not necessary that you already know the person. That's where the networking comes in.)

1. _____
2. _____
3. _____
4. _____
5. _____
6. _____
7. _____
8. _____
9. _____
10. _____
11. _____
12. _____
13. _____
14. _____
15. _____
16. _____

Think of three ways for you to approach each person on your list. You could include making an appointment to meet with the person, inviting an individual out to lunch, or attending a community event at which a person is likely to be.

1. _____
   a. _____
   b. _____
   c. _____
2. _____
   a. _____
   b. _____
   c. _____
3. _____
   a. _____
   b. _____
   c. _____
4. _____
   a. _____
   b. _____
   c. _____
5. _____
   a. _____
   b. _____
   c. _____
6. _____
   a. _____
   b. _____
   c. _____

(Continued)

7. _____

　　a. _____

　　b. _____

　　c. _____

8. _____

　　a. _____

　　b. _____

　　c. _____

9. _____

　　a. _____

　　b. _____

　　c. _____

10. _____

　　a. _____

　　b. _____

　　c. _____

11. _____

　　a. _____

　　b. _____

　　c. _____

12. _____

　　a. _____

　　b. _____

　　c. _____

13. _____

    a. _____

    b. _____

    c. _____

14. _____

    a. _____

    b. _____

    c. _____

15. _____

    a. _____

    b. _____

    c. _____

16. _____

    a. _____

    b. _____

    c. _____

Last, choose one strategy that you will implement for each person on your list. Then set a deadline for the accomplishment of that strategy.

1. _____

   Deadline: _____

2. _____

   Deadline: _____

3. _____

   Deadline: _____

4. _____

   Deadline: _____

5. _____

   Deadline: _____

6. _____

   Deadline: _____

7. _____

   Deadline: _____

8. _____

   Deadline: _____

9. _____

   Deadline: _____

10. _____

    Deadline: _____

11. _____

    Deadline: _____

12. _____

    Deadline: _____

13. _____

    Deadline: _____

14. _____

    Deadline: _____

15. _____

    Deadline: _____

16. _____

    Deadline: _____

GETTING INVOLVED

Networking is a lot like scoring points in a hockey game. Players know that the more shots they take, the better their chances are of scoring a goal. The same is true for you.

The more you are out meeting people, talking to them on the phone, or communicating with them through e-mail, the better chances you'll have of finding those meaningful relationships that will assist you in becoming successful. So get involved!

Join a college organization, an academic club, or a religious group. Meet people with similar interests in the business or social communities. For example, if you are an aspiring artist, you might find out the organizations to which your local museum curator belongs. Community involvement sends a clear message that you care about where you live. When you are involved in the community, you'll achieve visibility. Other people who are concerned and who care will take notice. You'll find that your involvement will not only benefit you in terms of networking and making connections but will benefit the community, too. That's the heart of win/win.

VOLUNTEERING

At the heart of community involvement is the idea of giving back in appreciation for all you have. In addition to giving back, you will also gain. You will increase your community contacts and develop personal and business relationships.

Think about those who actively participate in most not-for-profit volunteer groups within any community. Who are they? The majority are individuals holding executive level positions who bear impressive professional credentials. Imagine trying to get past the gatekeepers in the plush offices over which these executives rule. Ordinarily, someone just off-the-street can't do it! But if you are a volunteer, you can!

Volunteering levels the playing field. Around the conference table of a not-for-profit organization you will find people at the top of their careers, those just starting out, and individuals who fall somewhere in between. But in their roles as volunteers, each person is an equal. Each person has a chance to express ideas and opinions, and each person is listened to by the others. There is no better way to showcase your skills and abilities and to demonstrate your passions for what you truly believe in than as a volunteer. Not only will you give back something to the community, but you will grow your talents and be brought to the attention of others who will want to assist you in your career growth and your current employment. You can take your career to new heights.

To volunteer, first review your values and beliefs that you identified throughout the exercises in Chapter One. Then make a list of five community projects in which you strongly believe. You might want to volunteer in your community's food pantry or become involved a health association such as the American Red Cross or the American Cancer Society. You might decide to become a tutor in an elementary school. Use the following space to list the projects that appeal most to you.

I FEEL STRONGLY ABOUT THESE COMMUNITY PROJECTS

■ *PURPOSE:* To identify community efforts that you can become involved in.

1. _____
_____
_____
_____

2. _____
_____
_____
_____

3. _____
_____
_____
_____

4. _____
_____
_____
_____

5. _____
_____
_____
_____

After you have reviewed your values and beliefs and have identified appropriate community projects, the next step is to contact the local volunteer center or the agency you are interested in joining. Most communities have volunteer centers that will assist you in finding an organization with which you could build a relationship. Check your local telephone book for names and addresses of organizations and then list the information in the space provided.

ORGANIZATIONS I WILL CONTACT

1. Name: _____

   Address: _____

   Telephone Number: _____

   Contact Person: _____

   Date I Made Contact: _____

   Result: _____

   _____

2. Name: _____

   Address: _____

   Telephone Number: _____

   Contact Person: _____

   Date I Made Contact: _____

   Result: _____

   _____

(Continued)

3. Name: _____

Address: _____

Telephone Number: _____

Contact Person: _____

Date I Made Contact: _____

Result: _____

_____

4. Name: _____

Address: _____

Telephone Number: _____

Contact Person: _____

Date I Made Contact: _____

Result: _____

_____

5. Name: _____

Address: _____

Telephone Number: _____

Contact Person: _____

Date I Made Contact: _____

Result: _____

_____

Choose one or two of the projects to which you might devote your time and enter the volunteer arena with passion. With volunteering, you go forth with a passion that you're doing something right and making a contribution to the community. The community benefits, the organization benefits, and you benefit!

APPRECIATING THOSE WHO MAKE SUCCESS A LITTLE EASIER

*E*verybody likes to know that their efforts are appreciated, so take the time to show your thanks to those who make your success a little easier. The simplest way to do this is by hand writing thank-you notes.

Set a goal of sending three thank-you notes every week. Send a note to each person you meet, to each person you speak with on the phone, to each person who gives you a job lead, to each person who provides a referral. Become a thank-you note nut! What you'll find is that people will remember that you cared enough to thank them.

To get you started, here are thank-you note samples that you can use in four common career-building instances when thank-you notes are appropriate.

1. *Telephone Contact Thank You.* I appreciated the time you spent talking with me on the telephone. Time is such a precious resource in today's business world that I wanted to thank you for your generosity. I will keep you posted as I move forward with the suggestions you provided to me. Thank you again.

2. *In-Person Contact Thank You.* I appreciated your taking the time to meet with me. I so enjoyed meeting you, and I thank you for the time we shared in fruitful conversation. I gained a good deal of information about

the industry, and I appreciated all your insight and advice. Thank you again for taking time to see me.

3. *Job Lead Thank You.* I appreciated the job lead you shared with me. I have sent my resume to (name of company) and am awaiting word about setting up an interview. Thank you for thinking of me regarding this opportunity. I will keep you posted on my success with (name of company).

4. *Referral Thank You.* I appreciated your referral to (name of person) at (name of company). I spoke with Mr./Ms. (name) today, and I will be meeting him/her on Friday for an interview. I could not have made this marvelous contact without your assistance, and I thank you. I will let you know the results of our meeting.

■ **PURPOSE:** To identify those who have helped you recently.

In the space provided, list the names of three people who have done something for you in the past few weeks. The favor can be big or small. For example, the professor who spent some extra time preparing you for a final or the career counselor who edited your resumé.

1. _____

2. _____

3. _____

Purchase a package of blank thank-you notes. Write a short note to each of the above three people. Use the previous samples as guides and use the space provided to produce a rough draft of each note. Take the time to let each person know what their favor meant to you.

Note #1 _____

_____

_____

_____

_____

_____

_____

_____

_____

(Continued)

Note #2 _____

_____

_____

_____

_____

_____

_____

_____

_____

Note #3 _____

_____

_____

_____

_____

_____

_____

_____

_____

Continue to thank at least three people a week. With a stockpile of thank-you notes, set aside an hour to thank the individuals who have impacted your life positively. Don't wait. Go ahead and start now!

As you come to the end of this chapter, reflect on the success that is possible through networking. Formal and informal networking events allow you to achieve mutually beneficial business opportunities. By being open to those opportunities, you can promote yourself and your goals by taking action, getting involved in community groups or volunteer activities, and by appreciating those who make your success a little easier.

Now step into Chapter Five where your focus is success on the job—your next step on your journey of a thousand miles.

Read All About It!

Boe, Anne, & Bettie B. Youngs. *Is Your "Net" Working?: A Complete Guide to Building Contacts and Career Visibility.* New York, NY: John Wiley and Sons, 1989.

Bunkley, Crawford B. *The African American Network: Get Connected To More Than 5,000 Prominent People and Organizations in the African-American Community.* New York, NY: Plume, 1996.

Fraser, George C., George MacDonald Fraser, & Les Brown. *Success Runs In Our Race: The Complete Guide to Effective Networking in the African American Community.* New York, NY: William Morrow and Company, 1994.

Hadley, Joyce, and Betsy Sheldon. *The Smart Woman's Guide To Networking.* Broomall, PA: Chelsea House, 1997.

Holtz, Lou. *Winning Every Day.* New York, NY: Harper Business, 1998.

Kramer, Marc. *Power Networking: Using the Contacts You Don't Even Know You Have To Succeed in the Job You Want.* Lincolnwood, IL: VGM Career Horizons, 1997.

Krannich, Ronald L., & Caryl Rae Krannich. *Dynamite Networking For Dynamite Jobs: 101 Interpersonal, Telephone, and Electronic Techniques For Getting Job Leads, Interviews and Offers.* Manassas Park, VA: Impact Publications, 1996.

Mackay, Harvey. *Dig Your Well Before You're Thirsty: The Only Networking Book You'll Ever Need.* New York, NY: Doubleday, 1997.

Mandell, Terri. *Power Schmoozing: The New Etiquette for Social and Business Success.* New York, NY: McGraw-Hill, 1996.

Roane, Susan. *The Secrets of Savvy Networking: How To Make The Best Connection for Business and Personal Success.* New York, NY: Warner Books, 1993.

Tullier, L. Michelle. *Networking For Everyone: Connecting With People For Career and Job Success.* Indianapolis, IN: Just Works, 1998.

Vilas, Donna, Sandy Vilas, & Donna Fisher. *Power Networking: 55 Secrets for Personal and Professional Success.* Austin, TX: Mountainharbour Publications, 1992.

Books I've Read

Use the space provided to list the books you've read in this subject area and to reflect on what you've learned from reading them.

1. _____
2. _____
3. _____
4. _____
5. _____

Internet Resources

Use a search engine and the following key words to find information related to topics in this chapter: **networking, win/win, volunteering**.

My Favorite Internet Sites

Use the space provided to list your favorite Internet sites.

1. _____

2. _____

3. _____

4. _____

5. _____

Career Success Notes

SUCCESS On the Job

Excellence is at the heart of success on the job. When your family and friends support your vision, when you have the right on-the-job attitude, when you dress professionally, when you hone your communication skills, and when you manage your time, you're on your way to excellence.

After completing this chapter, you should understand:

- how to obtain support for your job
- how to cultivate the right on-the-job attitude
- how to dress professionally
- how to enhance the basic communication skills of listening, speaking, and writing
- how to manage your time

Your first day on a new job is both exciting and terrifying. You're eager to start, but you wonder how you'll fit in and if your skills can cut it in the real world. Take a deep breath then jump in with both feet. You're going to be terrific!

> *The secret of joy in work is contained in one word—excellence. To know how to do something well is to enjoy it.*
>
> PEARL BUCK,
> AMERICAN
> NOVELIST

OBTAINING SUPPORT
FOR YOUR VISION

You want to do the best you can on your new job because your performance will help you attain the goals you've set for yourself. One way that you can make sure that you do the best you can is to enlist the support of your family and friends.

Share with those close to you the goals you've established and the steps that you must take to realize those goals. When your family and friends realize how serious you are about attaining your objectives, they'll probably do whatever they can to support your efforts.

Maybe you need two hours of quiet time in the evening to work on a project. If you let your family know this, they might try to keep the noise level down or maybe they could make plans to be away from the house during that time.

When you socialize with friends, they'll probably ask how your job is going or ask about the progress you've made on your goals. Be honest. Friends can provide wonderful feedback—"Gee, it sounds like you're doing great!"—and can also give you encouragement when you need it—"Things are hectic now, but you'll get through it. Just hang in there!" And if they're really good friends, they may even give you a kick in the pants if they think you need one.

Having support for your job and for your goals will mean a lot when the going gets tough. It means you'll always have someone to turn to. It means you're all in this together.

KNOWING THE REQUIREMENTS OF YOUR JOB

On your first day on the job, you must have a clear understanding of the job's requirements. Sure, you know what duties you have to perform, but knowing a job's requirements goes beyond that. If the following aren't discussed with you during the first day, talk to your boss about them pronto:

- What are your specific goals and objectives for the next six to twelve months? What specific results are you expected to deliver?

- What are the most important leadership skills required for success in this position?

- How will you be evaluated? By whom?

- Who are the critical people or groups that you will need to rely on to perform your job effectively?

Before you can do your job well, you need to know what the job requires. And you need to know that you are indeed doing well. Ask people for feedback on how things are going. Don't wait for a formal performance review. By then, it might be too late to make a course correction.

CULTIVATING THE RIGHT ON-THE-JOB ATTITUDE

Your on-the-job attitude is important because it contributes to how well you'll fit into the work environment and determines how happy and successful you'll be there. Have a good attitude, and your boss and colleagues will know that you're a great match for the job. Have a bad attitude, and you're likely to feel not only the hot wrath of your boss, but the cold shoulders of your colleagues, too. Consider these suggestions for cultivating the right on-the-job attitude:

■ *Observe the office environment.* You'll spend the first few days on the job figuring out who's who and how things operate. This will give you valuable clues about how to behave as you ease yourself into the new work environment. Research shows that groups tend to accept those who adopt their rules of behavior, or norms, and reject those who ignore them. So keep your eyes and ears open during your first week to find out, for example, the degree of formality in the office. Are workers on a first-name basis with higher-ups, or are managers addressed as Mr. or Ms.? You don't want to call the CEO Marie if everybody else calls her Mrs. Custy.

■ *Adjust your enthusiasm.* You can't wait to roll up your sleeves and get started because you just know you're going to whip that place into shape in no time. Or so you think. You're a young rookie, and even though you're smart and ambitious, you've got a lot to learn. Your first lesson is that you won't endear yourself to more seasoned employees by being an over-zealous know-it-all. So temper your enthusiasm—at least during the first week!

■ *Accept criticism positively.* Because you're new at the job, it's expected that you'll do work incorrectly, make mistakes, and blunder your way through a sometimes steep learning curve. When you receive feedback—also known as criticism—avoid the tendency to become defensive or withdrawn. Accept the criticism positively by (1) asking for specific information about what you did incorrectly; (2) thinking about what you've heard and giving yourself time to react and; (3) deciding whether the criticism is well-taken. If it is, consider what you can do to avoid making the mistake the next time.

■ *Obey working-hour rules.* If work starts at 8:30AM, be there at 8:15AM to get settled, grab a cup of coffee, and be ready to start on time. Same thing at the other end of the day—you work until close of business. Don't duck out early for, or return late from, lunch.

■ *Respect company policies.* Many companies have policies that prohibit making personal telephone calls on business time. Other companies have policies regarding proper business apparel for employees. These policies are usually set forth in an employee handbook. Make sure you get a copy from the personnel office. Familiarize yourself with the policies in place at your company, then respect and follow them.

ASSEMBLING A WORKING WARDROBE

Once you've read and understand the company's dress-code policies, you can begin putting together a working wardrobe. Observe the employees who look polished and follow their lead in building your own wardrobe. Not sure where to start? You may need the help of a personal shopper.

A personal shopper can help you find the right suit or business dress—even build an entire wardrobe within your budget—in less time than it would take for you to do it yourself. Does this sound like a service that only Donald Trump could afford? Wrong! Personal shopping services are sometimes offered free of charge at many department and specialty stores, and no minimum purchase is required.

Here's how it works. You make an appointment for a consultation with a store's personal shopper. After you tell the personal shopper about your definite likes and dislikes, he or she completes a computerized preference file for you containing information regarding sizes, favorite colors, styles, and designers as well as vital statistics such as name, address, phone number, birthdate, hair and eye color. You then describe the garments you're looking for, the desirable price range, and then you both hit the sales floor.

Julie Rosenthal

Banta Integrated Media

Just doing a job is not enough to ensure success, according to Julie Rosenthal of Banta Integrated Media. "It helps to become involved in the inner workings of the company," Rosenthal said. "I know that some people within the company who have moved up and who have done really well happen to be the people who are also involved in helping to establish company policies or making suggestions to supervisors on how to improve customer service."

In order to go these extra miles, Rosenthal believes it's important that a person take a job that he or she will enjoy. "People can tell when someone's not happy, and when you're not happy, it does rub off on your work," Rosenthal said. "If you're not enjoying what you're doing, you're not going to want to stay late; you're not going to want to help the company get ahead."

Although many job seekers think that being chosen by a company is important, Rosenthal believes that more important is the job seeker choosing the company. "You really want to be happy," Rosenthal said. "If you're enjoying what you're doing, then you're going to give more naturally."

For Rosenthal, that's a clear case of win/win.

> *I think the most important thing initially is to find out if they're interested in what we're doing because we don't want anybody who just wants a job, we want somebody who's going to be excited about our company.*

Why does it have to be a team deal? Mainly for your convenience. The personal shopper can make a beeline right to the appropriate merchandise, which cuts down on the time you have to spend shopping.

After making your selections, it's on to the fitting room. While you try on the clothes, the shopper heads back to the racks to choose other garments you might like. If you make any purchases, they are recorded on your preference file which becomes a reference tool for the shopper.

Once he or she knows your needs and preferences, your personal shopper will put things aside for you so you have first choice on new merchandise. A personal shopper also helps you save money by letting you know when clothing goes on sale. But there's never any pressure to buy. Most personal shoppers won't push for a sale because it's bad for business.

A personal shopper will also be honest with you. He or she won't sell you something you don't like because then he or she isn't being a friend to you. If you get home and you really dislike the suit, the personal shopper has done more harm than good.

Personal shoppers are not for everybody. If you're the type who never listens to anyone about fashion, then a personal shopper probably isn't for you. To make the most of one, you should be flexible and open to his or her suggestions. Try on red and black even if you always wear less striking colors. Don a dramatic coat instead of your usual leather biker jacket. When you're overhauling a basic jeans-and-tee-shirt wardrobe, experiment. Have fun reinventing yourself.

Think about your new image, then get busy buying the pieces you truly need. Today when it's so important to look your best, personal shopping is a service you can't afford to pass up.

Basic Communication Skills

Motivational expert Anthony Robbins believes that: "The level of success that you experience in life, the happiness, joy, love, external rewards, and impact that you create is the direct result of how you communicate to yourself and to others. The quality of your life is the quality of your communication." Your ability to communicate impacts your level of success on the job, too. At work, your ability to listen actively, to speak well, and to create clear written messages reflects not only on you but on the company you work for. That's why good communication skills are so important.

Communication can be verbal or nonverbal, and the goal of communication is to exchange messages. The message flows from a sender (the person who transmits the message) to the receiver (the person who gets the message). Communication is considered effective when both the sender and the receiver have a common understanding of the message. That means when you (the sender) telephone your friend (the receiver) and say "Let's go out for pizza tonight" (message), you both show up at the right place and the right time to split a pie. Even a simple message like this requires good speaking and listening skills.

Listening

Chapter Three discussed techniques for active listening during job interviews, including being prepared to listen, being open and curious, and asking questions. Once you're on the job, you'll need to take listening to the next level by focusing on "listening between the lines" or paying attention to nonverbal cues. Many nonverbal cues are things you see when you look at a speaker:

- *facial expressions*—smiling, frowning, raising eyebrows
- *eye contact*—looking downward, making direct eye contact, glancing away
- *body language*—yawning, tapping fingers or feet, gesturing with hands

These cues give you a sense of the speaker's feelings and unsaid messages, and they improve your ability to understand the message.

You can test by comparing a face-to-face conversation with a telephone conversation. Talking to someone in person lets you see the smile, the glancing away, and the hand gestures plus hear the voice. On the phone, you can only hear the voice, and that reduces your ability to understand the message. During the next few days, try the following exercise.

I'm Trying Hard to Hear You

■PURPOSE: To compare the effectiveness of a face-to-face conversation with a telephone conversation.

1. *Face-to-Face Conversation:* When a friend shares an opinion or feelings with you, listen with your ears *and* with your eyes. When your friend finishes speaking, say "Let me verify that I heard what you said. . ." and then say in your own words the message you think your friend communicated. Ask your friend to check the accuracy of your understanding. Use the space provided to write a short paragraph about your experience, indicating how close your understanding of the message was to your friend's actual message. If differences occurred, why do you think they happened?

   _____

   _____

   _____

   _____

   _____

2. *Telephone Conversation:* When a friend shares an opinion or feelings with you, listen with your ears. When your friend finishes speaking, say "Let me verify that I heard what you said. . ." and then say in your own words the message you think your friend communicated. Ask your friend to check the accuracy of your understanding. Use the space provided to write a short paragraph about your experience, indicating how close your understanding of the message was to your friend's actual message. If differences occurred, why do you think they happened?

   _____

   _____

   _____

   _____

   _____

SPEAKING

*T*hink of all the ways you communicate on the job by speaking. You give directions, ask and answer questions, explain procedures, share your ideas in meetings, and talk on the telephone.

While people get their first impression of you from your appearance, they get their second impression from how you speak. If you want people to think of you as intelligent and competent, you must speak well. To speak well you must:

- control the qualities of your voice—volume, pitch, rate, and tone

- pronounce words correctly and enunciate

- speak clearly

- use correct vocabulary and grammar

To determine how well you speak, tape record a conversation you have with a colleague. Play back the tape and listen to what your voice sounds like. Then ask a person you trust to listen to the tape and to evaluate how well you speak by using the following exercise.

How You Rate My Speech Qualities

■ **PURPOSE:** To evaluate speech qualities.

1. I speak standard English. ☐ Yes ☐ Sometimes ☐ No

2. I speak at a moderate volume (not too loud or too soft). ☐ Yes ☐ Sometimes ☐ No

3. I speak at a moderate pitch. ☐ Yes ☐ Sometimes ☐ No

4. I vary the pitch for different meanings. ☐ Yes ☐ Sometimes ☐ No

5. I use pauses to emphasize important points. ☐ Yes ☐ Sometimes ☐ No

6. I control the tone of my voice. ☐ Yes ☐ Sometimes ☐ No

7. I speak clearly and distinctly. ☐ Yes ☐ Sometimes ☐ No

8. I use a wide range of words when I speak. ☐ Yes ☐ Sometimes ☐ No

9. I pronounce words correctly when I speak. ☐ Yes ☐ Sometimes ☐ No

10. I use correct grammar when I speak. ☐ Yes ☐ Sometimes ☐ No

For any statements that are answered "No," refer to some of the books at the end of this section that can help you improve in those areas.

EFFECTIVE CONVERSATIONS

Speaking well is only one part of effective conversations. Along with knowing what it is you want to say, you must:

■ establish a good environment for the conversation

■ use body language correctly

■ listen actively

■ allow others to speak

That's a lot to pack into any conversation, but it all begins with the message—what you want to say. Be mentally prepared to deliver the goods by deciding the points you need to cover and your specific approach. Also keep in mind that in addition to knowing what you want to say, you have to remember what you don't want to say. You must respect confidences and be discreet and tactful. If not, people will view you as untrustworthy and rude. Not a reputation you want to have.

Establishing a good environment for the conversation means you encourage the free flow of communication. You eliminate barriers by coming from behind a large desk, you sit with a person who is seated, you rearrange the furniture to make the conversation comfortable.

You also use positive body language—smiling, maintaining eye contact, gesturing for emphasis. Avoid any mannerisms that can be distracting to the other person such as shifting an object from one hand to the other or knocking a pencil against a coffee cup.

You listen actively, and you allow others to speak. Since a conversation is a dialogue not a monologue, you'll want to pay attention to your listener. Listeners give cues that tell you when they want to say something. Mind the cues, complete your statement, yield the floor, and then listen in silence.

SPEAKING ON THE TELEPHONE

Since the visual dimension of the communication is missing, telephone conversations are challenging. You rely on your words and voice to send your message, and you have to concentrate on being courteous and attentive. Telephones, voice mail, and answering machines are integral parts of your job, so it pays to know how to use them in order to make your communications more effective.

- *When you place a call,* greet the other person and identify yourself. For example: "Good morning! This is Peter Hess from YAPA®." This eliminates confusion for the person on the other end of the line, since he or she doesn't have to try to guess who you are from the sound of your voice.

- *Speak directly into the mouthpiece of the telephone,* keeping your mouth about an inch from the phone. If the phone slips below your chin, the listener won't be able to hear you clearly, or your voice may not record clearly on a voice mail system or an answering machine.

- *Don't shout!* Speak at a normal volume. If the person can't hear you, you might have a bad connection. Place the call again.

- *Speak clearly.* When stating important information, spell out words that your listener might misunderstand. For example: "Please make your check payable to Layne Enterprises. Layne is spelled L as in Larry, A as in apple, Y as in yellow, N as in Nancy, and E as in Edward."

- *Be courteous* with the words you use and the tone of your voice. Remember to say "please" and "thank you," and to keep your voice pleasant and friendly.

- *Be attentive.* Acknowledge that you are paying attention by saying "Yes" or "I understand."

- *If you have to step away from the phone,* excuse yourself from the listener and then put the call on hold.

■ *Avoid dropping the receiver or banging it on your desk.* The noise will be amplified for the person at the other end of the line. Replace the receiver in its cradle gently when you hang up.

■ *When using a speaker phone,* place the unit in front of you so that your voice will be picked up properly.

■ *Have a pad of paper and a pencil near the telephone* in case you reach a voice-mail system instead of a person. You can jot down the menu choices, so you can be sure to choose the best one: "For account balances, press 2."

■ *When leaving a voice-mail message,* be brief and to the point. A good rule of thumb these days is to be prepared to leave a voice-mail message before you make a call. This will help you to be concise if you should get the person's voice-mail box.

■ *What you say can and will be used against you!* Remember that voice mail is no different than a memo. It can be saved and filed, so be careful of what you say. This is especially true when leaving messages for your peers and friends. Many organizations have personnel who check voice-mail messages when others are out of town. So you don't want to say anything that could embarrass you or cause problems for your friends.

■ *If you get lost in an automated telephone system,* remember to press 0 to be put through to a human being.

■ *For your own voice mail,* keep your recorded message brief, up-to-date, and professional. Some companies require employees to update their voice mail daily so that callers will know whether or not to expect a return call that day.

■ *Check your voice mail frequently and return calls promptly.* Treat your calls as if each came from your boss.

WRITING

*L*etters, memos, e-mail messages, reports, and the like are all part of the writing tasks you'll do on the job. Are your written messages confusing and incomplete? Do you tend to overwrite? Does your boss go berserk with a red pencil on any written material you turn in? If so, do you fear that you'll have to repeat English 101? Relax! Writing is a skill that can be developed without going back to the classroom.

A classic book on the subject is *The Elements of Style* by William Strunk, Jr. and E.B. White. Buy this book! This little gem will refresh your memory about usage rules, principles of composition, and an approach to style.

Once you recall the basics, apply the rules to the next memo you have to write. Then, as long as you're not on a deadline, put the memo aside for a day or two. When you go back to the memo after two days, read it through carefully. Put a mark in the margin next to anything that does not seem quite correct. Then pick up *The Elements of Style* and figure out how you can make the memo better. The secret to good writing is in re-writing, and *The Elements of Style* can make your writing sparkle.

Follow the same basic rules when writing e-mail messages but add a few for this special medium of communication:

■ *Maintain a professional tone in all business-related e-mail.* Treat e-mail as a formal, written letter. You never know who'll be printing and saving the message or checking your grammar and punctuation. If you're even considering sending an e-mail that can be construed as contentious or creating conflict, think again! If in doubt, don't send the e-mail; talk to the person first.

■ *Be brief.* People are very busy, and some receive hundreds of e-mail messages a day. Edit your e-mails so that they're brief and to the point.

Use emoticons when appropriate. Emoticons are communication elements inserted in e-mail as a form of short-hand to represent phrases or to express emotions that may not come through in the words themselves. Some commonly used emoticons include:

BTW	By The Way
CAM	Couldn't Agree More
FWIW	For What It's Worth
FYI	For Your Information
GMTA	Great Minds Think Alike
ICBW	I Could Be Wrong
IMO	In My Opinion
IMHO	In My Humble Opinion
IMNSHO	In My *Not* So Humble Opinion
IOW	In Other Words
ITA	I Totally Agree
JMO	Just My Opinion
JMHO	Just My Humble Opinion
LOL	Laughing Out Loud
OTOH	On The Other Hand
<G>	Grin
<BG>	Big Grin
<VBG>	Very Big Grin

:-) or =) or :)	Smiley Face (Happy)
:-D	Huge Grin (Very Happy)
:-(	Sad Face (Disappointment)
:-O	Surprise!!!
<S>	Big Smile
:>	Little Grin
;-)	Wink
=(	Very Sad

■ *Read the message at least twice before hitting the "Send" button.* Does the message say what you want? Can any of the words be misinterpreted? Is the tone professional and appropriate? Once you've sent a message, there's no way to get it back.

■ *Be polite.* Remember that you never know where an e-mail message will end up. Be proud to have that document in someone's file folder somewhere. Remember, too, that even though you delete e-mail from your directory, the message is still in your company's system and can be retrieved. Make certain that your e-mail doesn't contain anything you wouldn't want a third-party to see.

Managing Your Time

"*T*hose who make the worst use of their time are the first to complain of its shortness," according to 17th century French writer Jean La Bruyere. Things may have been busy back then, but they're turbocharged today, and people complain more than ever about time as a dwindling natural resource. True, you can't control the passage of time, but you can take action to control your use of time.

Do you put things off? Do you complain about not having enough time for all you have to do? Do you waste or misuse time? If so, time management can help you overcome these obstacles to accomplishing your goals.

Procrastination

*C*hapter One characterized procrastination as a pothole in the road to success. People who put things off are called procrastinators. Many procrastinators delay tasks because they fear failure. They don't know how the task will turn out, and this uncertainty causes increased stress. So instead of plunging into the project, they come up with excuses for not starting it.

Other procrastinators think that making a decision to undertake a task is just as good as completing the task. They decide to work on a paper for a literature class but then reason that they'll go to the mall first and write the paper later. Somehow the paper doesn't get written.

Some people are happy to live their lives as procrastinators. If you have a tendency to put things off, and you're unhappy with the fact that you're not meeting your goals, make a decision right now to overcome procrastination.

Once you banish procrastination from your life, you'll start a task on time, work on it steadily, and finish it on time. You'll gain a feeling of control over projects. You'll meet rather than miss deadlines, you'll keep your stress level low, and you'll get things done. Think of the rush of satisfaction you'll feel when you complete a difficult project. What a feeling!

Beat procrastination by putting into practice these strategies for any task you've been putting off:

■ *Set a deadline.* Decide when a task needs to be completed and use that as your deadline date. Circle that date on your calendar in red.

■ *Break the task into its component parts.* You wouldn't eat a six-foot sub in one sitting would you? No! You'd probably cut it up in sections and eat one section every day. It's the same thing with huge projects. Tackle your huge project one section at a time. Make a list of all the project's component parts and do one part at a time. The momentum you'll build along the way will keep you moving through the entire project.

■ *Establish a start date.* Overwhelming projects that require a lot of effort need more than just a deadline for completing them. Look at all of the parts of your project that must be done and decide how long each part will take. Then, working back from your deadline, figure out when you need to start the project in order to finish it on time. Circle that date on your calendar in blue.

■ *Start with something easy.* If the task is tough, ease yourself into the project by starting with something easy. Once you've begun, you can shift into the harder parts of the task. The Roman poet Horace said it best: "He who has begun has half done."

■ *Schedule progressive rewards.* For a large task, reward yourself for accomplishing various sections. Save one big reward for completing the entire task.

"I JUST DON'T HAVE ENOUGH TIME!"

Perhaps you don't procrastinate. Maybe you complain that you just don't have enough time for all you have to do, including family, household, school, work, and community responsibilities. There's an old saying that if you need something done, ask a busy person to do it. Busy people realize that we all have the same number of hours each week: 7 days a week x 24 hours day = 168 hours, and they make the most of those hours. How do you use your hours? If you'd like to find out, use the following exercise.

HOW I SPEND MY TIME

■ **PURPOSE:** To identify how you use your time over the course of a week.

For the next week, use the following time log to record how you spend your time. List all activities, including commuting, running errands, watching television, and leisure time.

My Time Log

Time	Monday	Tuesday	Wednesday
7:00AM			
8:00AM			
9:00AM			
10:00AM			
11:00AM			
12:00NOON			
1:00PM			
2:00PM			
3:00PM			
4:00PM			
5:00PM			
6:00PM			
7:00PM			
8:00PM			
9:00PM			
10:00PM			
11:00PM			
12:00MIDNIGHT			
1:00AM			
2:00AM			
3:00AM			
4:00AM			
5:00AM			
6:00AM			

Week of _____

Thursday	Friday	Saturday	Sunday

WASTING AND MISUSING TIME

*P*eople who complain about not having enough time for all they have to do often suffer from the twin problems of wasting time and misusing time. They waste time by slow-poking their way through projects, and they misuse time by spending too much of it on unimportant tasks and not enough of it on tasks that are significant. They end up spending days focused on trivial matters with no time left for the things that really matter to them. Don't let this happen to you! Use the following exercise to see how well you use your time.

HOW WELL I USE MY TIME

■ **PURPOSE:** To identify how well you use your time.

Review the time log you kept for one week then complete the following:

1. The total number of hours I spent on these activities:

   Sleeping: _____

   Eating: _____

   Working: _____

   Classes: _____

   Commuting: _____

   Studying: _____

   Chores: _____

   Exercising/Recreation: _____

   Socializing: _____

   Watching TV: _____

   Goofing Off: _____

   Other: _____

   Total should be 168 hours.

2. The total number of hours I spent on worthwhile activities:

   _____

3. The total number of hours I spent on meaningless or trivial activities:

   _____

   (Continued)

4. The activities I wish I had spent more time on are:

_____

_____

_____

_____

_____

_____

5. The activities I wish I had spent less time on are:

_____

_____

_____

_____

_____

_____

6. The activities that I wanted to do but didn't get around to doing during the week are:

_____

_____

_____

_____

_____

_____

Managing Your Time

*P*arkinson's Law states that "work expands so as to fill the time available for its completion." In the past, you've probably experienced the results of this law, but now you probably realize now that without some sort of time management system, your time will evaporate. If you allow procrastination, not having enough time, wasting and misusing time to eat away at your days, you will have lived a life without accomplishing any of your goals. Be in control of your life! Achieve your goals! Take charge of your time!

Being Organized is Key

*B*eing organized means you keep your goals in mind and you plan the accomplishment of those goals in advance. You practiced being organized in Chapter One when you created short-, intermediate-, and long-term goals. You probably remember that planning comes before action, which is why you set up a plan for achieving the goals you set. As you developed your action plan, you decided what you want to do; the resources you need to do it; and the steps you must take to achieve it. That's great! But you probably have more than one goal. How do you decide what you will spend your time on? You do that by setting priorities.

When you set priorities, you decide the tasks that are most important and which must be done first. Review everything you need to do and then allocate your tasks to one of the following categories:

1. The tasks that must be done immediately are:

2. The tasks that are important to do soon are:

3. The tasks that can be delayed for a few days are:

4. The tasks that can be delayed for a week, a month, or longer are:

This system sets up your priorities. The tasks in categories #1 and #2 have the highest priority, and you should work on these first. The tasks in categories #3 and #4 have lower priority and can be done once you've accomplished the higher-priority objectives.

You'll find that establishing priorities helps you to isolate the most-urgent tasks associated with particular goals. Sometimes you must postpone working on one or more of your goals so that you can attain the others.

Practice setting priorities in the following exercise.

MY PRIORITIES FOR THE WEEK

■PURPOSE: To identify your highest priority activities for one week.

Make a list of all the things you have to do for the week ahead.

1. _____
2. _____
3. _____
4. _____
5. _____
6. _____
7. _____
8. _____
9. _____
10. _____
11. _____
12. _____
13. _____
14. _____
15. _____
16. _____

(Continued)

17. _____

18. _____

19. _____

20. _____

Review your list and assign each task a priority number from 1 to 4. Remember that #1 represents tasks that must be done without delay (highest priority); #2 represents tasks that should be done soon (important); #3 represents tasks that can be done next week (less important); #4 represents tasks that can be delayed for more than a week (least important).

Now allocate each task to its place in the exercise *My List of Tasks for the Week*.

MY LIST OF TASKS FOR THE WEEK

Week of: _____

1. The tasks that must be done immediately are:

_____

_____

_____

_____

2. The tasks that are important to do soon are:

_____

_____

_____

_____

3. The tasks that can be delayed for a few days are:

_____

_____

_____

_____

4. The tasks that can be delayed for a week, a month, or longer are:

_____

_____

_____

_____

TIME MANAGEMENT TOOLS

*O*nce you know your highest priorities, you can use time management tools to help you set up a schedule. Plug in your fixed daily activities such as working, attending class, sleeping, eating, etc., then use the time left over for your highest priority tasks.

When scheduling those tasks, be realistic about the time involved for each activity. For example, if you need to spend one hour at the library researching a project, figure in the travel time to and from the library. If it takes you thirty minutes to get to the library, you'll need to allocate two hours for the research project (1 hour research time + 1 hour for round-trip travel).

Be aware of your peak energy levels throughout the day. Some people have high energy in the morning and are dragging by afternoon. Other people have to be blasted out of bed in the morning, but by afternoon they are going at full throttle. Schedule hard or important tasks for the times during the day when your energy is at its peak.

YOUR PLANNER

*T*ime management tools, also called planners, are calendars in a variety of formats that help you schedule your life weeks and months in advance. Head to your local office supply store to check out the different types, styles, and sizes of planning systems that are available.

Select your system wisely. Since the planner will be your only source of information about your work, school, and social schedules, the system should have enough room for you to write and be a convenient size for you to carry with you. Some planners offer both paper-based and computer-based systems. Choose whichever type works the best for your lifestyle.

Many planners allow you to schedule intermediate- and long-term activities as well as to keep a daily "to do" list. Your "to do" list is the way you get things done that contribute to your intermediate- and long-term goals.

Get into the habit of creating your list the night before and itemizing all of the tasks that need doing during that day. Prioritize the tasks in A-B-C order with A-tasks being those of highest priority. If you have four A-tasks, you can further prioritize them by assigning A-1, A-2, A-3, and A-4 order to them. Consult your list during the day so that you know what you have to do, and cross items off your "to do" list when you've completed those tasks.

Use the following weekly planner to practice making time commitments for the next week. Start by entering your fixed daily activities such as working, attending class, sleeping, eating, etc.

MY WEEKLY PLANNER

■**PURPOSE:** To practice making time commitments for a week.

Complete the planner on the following pages.

My Weekly Planner

Time	Monday	Tuesday	Wednesday
7:00AM			
8:00AM			
9:00AM			
10:00AM			
11:00AM			
12:00NOON			
1:00PM			
2:00PM			
3:00PM			
4:00PM			
5:00PM			
6:00PM			
7:00PM			
8:00PM			
9:00PM			
10:00PM			
11:00PM			
12:00MIDNIGHT			
1:00AM			
2:00AM			
3:00AM			
4:00AM			
5:00AM			
6:00AM			

Week of _____

Thursday	Friday	Saturday	Sunday

Now use the following space to create a "to do" list of all the tasks you want to accomplish tomorrow. After you've listed them, assign each task a priority number from 1 to 4. Remember that #1 represents tasks that must be done without delay (highest priority); #2 represents tasks that should be done soon (important); #3 represents tasks that can be done next week (less important); #4 represents tasks that can be delayed for more than a week (least important).

To Do List

1. _____

2. _____

3. _____

4. _____

5. _____

6. _____

7. _____

8. _____

9. _____

10. _____

Estimate the amount of time each of your highest priority tasks will take then list these tasks on the appropriate day of *My Weekly Planner*. As you complete your tasks, cross them off your "to do" list.

STRATEGIES FOR MANAGING YOUR TIME

*B*enjamin Franklin wrote: "You may delay, but time will not." When you adopt time management tools that work for you, you'll be amazed at how easy it is to organize yourself and to make plans, schedules, and lists. But did you plan for the unexpected? That's hard to do, which is why time-planning tools often go out the window when life throws a curve ball that introduces interruptions to your schedule.

If you want to harness the true power of effective time management, you must learn to be organized and flexible. That means you can handle interferences to your schedule, meet the demands of others, learn to say no when your time is already spoken for, and become skilled at using bits and pieces of time to your advantage.

MEETING THE DEMANDS OF OTHERS

*U*nless you live and work in a cave, you're surrounded by people, such as friends, family, and colleagues, who care about you and want some of your time and attention. Do you shut them out of your life just so you can maintain your schedule? No! You plan time in your schedule for socializing.

But what should you do when, even though you've planned social time, people interrupt you at other times? Simple—just plan to be interrupted. Build response time into your schedule by planning more time than you think a given task will take. In that way, you'll have plenty of time to finish a task by your deadline despite interruptions.

JUST SAY NO

*R*ealizing that you have only 168 hours a week to work with, you need to develop the ability to say "no" to extra projects or demands that will lead to overcommitting yourself. Explain to others who try to push the projects or make the demands that what you have already scheduled is important and that additional responsibilities have to take a number.

Now this will be difficult to explain to your boss, and that's where your time management tool comes to the rescue. When your boss comes into your office to toss more work into your in-basket, ask him or her for a few minutes of time to discuss priorities.

Have available your time management tools and plans to share with your boss the work time commitments you already have scheduled. Then sort through the additional work that was placed into your in-basket. Ask your boss for help in prioritizing the new work. Your boss may realize that you are overcommitted presently and agree to shift the new work to a less-hectic time. Or your boss may think that the new work is more important than your current projects and make the new work a higher priority. Whichever scenario plays out, you will continue to work on the highest priority projects, and you will not have your stress level rise because you have too much to do.

USING BITS AND PIECES OF TIME

*O*ccasionally, you will be presented with unexpected bits and pieces of time. Maybe a meeting gets out ten minutes early or perhaps a client cancels a one-hour appointment. What do you do with these bits and pieces? You use them.

When presented with such luxuries as extra time, immediately ask yourself: "What is the best use of this time right now?" Spend the time with small tasks such as catching up with your reading, getting some exercise, or starting a project. If you're an effective time manager you won't just kill time, you'll work it to death!

As you come to the end of this chapter, consider the many factors involved in achieving success on the job. You need the support of family and friends, the right on-the-job attitude, and the right professional look. You need good communication skills in the areas of listening, speaking, and writing. You need to manage your time in order to reach your potential and to achieve your goals.

You're almost there, so keep going! Step into Chapter Six where you'll look at achieving success for life.

Read All About It!

Axelrod, Alan & Jim Holtje. *201 Ways to Manage Your Time Better.* New York, NY: McGraw-Hill, 1997.

Benjamin, Susan. *Words At Work: Business Writing in Half the Time With Twice the Power.* Reading, MA: Addison-Wesley, 1997.

Booher, Dianna Daniels. *Get a Life Without Sacrificing Your Career: How To Make More Time For What's Really Important.* New York, NY: McGraw-Hill, 1996.

Covey, Stephen, A. Roger Merrill, & Rebecca R. Merrill. *First Things First.* New York, NY: Simon and Schuster, 1994.

Gelb, Michael J. & Bradley L. Winch. *Present Yourself! Captivate Your Audience with Great Presentation Skills.* Rolling Hills Estates, CA: Jalmar Press, 1988.

Helgesen, Marc, & Steve Brown. *Active Listening: Building Skills for Understanding.* New York, NY: Cambridge University Press, 1994.

Matthews, Candace & Phillip Edmondson. *Speaking Solutions: Interaction, Presentation, Listening, and Pronunciation Skills.* Upper Saddle River, NJ: Prentice Hall, 1994.

Moreno, Mary. *The Writer's Guide to Corporate Communications.* New York, NY: Allworth Press, 1997.

Morrisey, George L., Thomas L. Sechrest, & Wendy B. Warman. *Loud and Clear: How To Prepare and Deliver Effective Business and Technical Presentations.* Reading, MA: Addison-Wesley, 1997.

Numrich, Carol. *Consider the Issues: Advanced Listening and Critical Thinking Skills.* Reading, MA: Addison-Wesley, 1995.

Strunk, William, & E. B. White. *The Elements of Style.* 3rd ed. Needham Heights, MA: Allyn & Bacon, 1995.

Swenson, Jack, & Elaine Brett. *The Building Blocks of Business Writing: The Foundation of Writing Skills.* Los Altos, CA: Crisp Publications, 1991.

Ratliffe, Sharon A., & David D. Hudson. *Communication for Everyday Living: Integrating Basic Speaking, Listening and Thinking Skills.* Upper Saddle River, NJ: Prentice Hall, 1989.

Venolia, Jan. *Rewrite Right: How To Revise Your Way to Better Writing.* Berkeley, CA: Ten Speed Press, 1987.

Williamson, Sarah. *Stop, Look and Listen: Using Your Senses From Head to Toe.* Charlotte, VT: Williamson Publishers, 1996.

Young, Pam, & Peggy Jones. *Get Your Act Together! A 7-Day Get-Organized Program For the Overworked, Overbooked, and Overwhelmed.* New York, NY: HarperCollins Publishers, 1993.

Books I've Read

Use the space provided to list the books you've read in this subject area and to reflect on what you've learned from reading them.

1. _____

2. _____

3. _____

4. _____

5. _____

Internet Resources

http://cbpa.louisville.edu/bruce/mgt301/listen.htm

This site contains links to listening resources such as listening in the classroom and listening as a parent.

http://www.eslcafe.com/search/Speaking/

Dave's ESL Cafe is a site with links to English-as-a-Second-Language resources on the Internet.

http://www.columbia.edu/cu/healthwise/0616.html

The Columbia University Health Service provides tips on overcoming procrastination.

My Favorite Internet Sites

Use the space provided to list your favorite Internet sites.

1. _____

2. _____

3. _____

4. _____

5. _____

Career Success Notes

SUCCESS for Life

The true measure of success is your own vision of a ful-filled life. Whatever your dreams may be, measure your success not by how far away you are from your goal but by how many steps you've taken toward your goal. With enough momentum—gathered from working with mentors, being a life-long learner, and creating building blocks of commitment—you'll cease creeping along the path, and you'll soar to success. This chapter is your launching pad.

After completing this chapter, you should understand:

- how mentors assist in achieving goals

- how to find and work with a mentor

- how to become a mentor

- how life-long learning contributes to life-long success

- how to create building blocks of commitment to success

> **N**ever consent to creep when you feel an impulse to soar.
>
> HELEN KELLER,
> AMERICAN
> AUTHOR, LECTURER,
> HUMANITARIAN

Success is not a result or an ending point. It's a way of life. The way in which you go about moving toward your goals is important.

If your life goal is to become the chief executive officer of a large international company, don't be disappointed if you're not offered the job on your first day of work. You need to be prepared for reality, especially the reality of the corporate world where patience is not only a virtue, it's also a prerequisite for the job.

Reality also means that much hard work is ahead of you. But if you're determined, if you'll let nothing stand in your way, you will successfully reach the end of the road. You have signposts to guide your journey—mentors, life-long learning, and building blocks of commitment—so hold fast to your goals and keep your eye on the prize. You're on your way.

HOW MENTORS ASSIST IN ACHIEVING GOALS

Think about the idea of having a role model in your life for the "you" of the future. Imagine sitting down with this person to discuss your goals, dreams, and career plans and having this individual offer information, references, and guidance based on years of experience. This person—your mentor—is your ally in achieving your goals.

Mentors understand the industry, their part in the organization, and they have a great deal to teach you. If you are open to learning, mentors can share the things they did right, the mistakes they made along the way, and the benefit of their wisdom to help you avoid the same errors.

Your mentor could be your boss, a colleague, a business partner, a friend, a parent, even a competitor. As you grow in your career and begin to network outside of your familiar surroundings, you'll meet many individuals who will bring an inspirational or educational influence to your life. Don't feel frustrated now if you have no one in your life who you feel fits the mentor mold. You've only begun to meet potential mentors.

As you grow professional and personally, you will be amazed at how your appetite for knowledge and your thirst for education will grow. What will also increase is your need for new mentors to support you as you enter new areas of your life.

You can have different mentors for various aspects of your career and/or personal life. You can even have the mentoring equivalent of a board of directors—multiple mentors from both inside and outside your company. You might also change mentors, depending on where you are in your professional development. From some mentors you may want inspiration and motivation; from others you may want discipline.

That's right, discipline. The best kind of mentor is one you will want to not disappoint. The best thing you can do for yourself is to tell your mentor exactly what you want in life. The funny thing about doing this is that afterwards, you'll feel that you don't want to let your mentor down.

It's very easy to let yourself down. Who is going to know other than you? But if you tell a few people about your dreams and your vision, you'll have a much harder time explaining to them about your subsequent lack of progress. To avoid having to do that, you'll work harder, and you'll achieve success, and you'll be eager and proud to let your mentor know.

FINDING AND WORKING WITH A MENTOR

Rooted in ancient Greece, mentoring is a concept that's been given a modern-day spin by today's corporations. In Homer's *Odyssey*, when Odysseus left to fight the Trojan

War, he left his son Telemachus in the care of the tutor Mentor. Mentor later revealed her true identity—she was actually the Goddess Athena, patroness of the arts and industry—and went with Telemachus on his search for his missing father.

Similarly, your mentor should see you through thick and thin. But how do you find a mentor? Typically, you'll meet people who are potential mentors through work, as a result of your involvement in a business association, or through your community volunteer activities. (Are you starting to see how all of the topics discussed so far are starting to come together? That is why success is a lifestyle and not any one thing that you can put your finger on.)

You can also find a mentor on-line. Tapping into www.yapa.com offers you the opportunity to take part in an on-line mentor matching system with professionals in your field, human resources managers, and college professors.

Many companies today are also updating the traditional one-on-one mentoring relationship with formal or guided mentoring programs. Through these programs, women and minorities are matched with experienced, senior-level managers. Groups of protégés interact on a regular basis with a single mentor who may or may not be involved in the same department or business. In fact, the mentor may have very different talents and perspectives to bring to the table. This is called cross-skill mentoring, and as a result both the protégés and the mentor broaden their experiences and their knowledge bases.

In the years ahead, you'll find even more opportunities for formal or guided mentoring programs at companies interested in sharing so-called "intellectual capital." In fact, a 1996 survey conducted by *Human Resource Executive* magazine found that between 1995 and 1996 the percentage of businesses planning mentoring programs more than doubled from 17 percent to 36 percent. Major corporations that have jumped on the mentoring bandwagon include: AT&T, Merrill Lynch, Federal Express, General Motors, J.C. Penney, Bell Labs, DuPont, Sun Microsystems,

Charles Schwab, BellSouth Corp., Barnett Bank, Texas Commerce Bank, and scores of others.

When choosing your mentor, be on the lookout for someone you admire who is open, successful, and someone you feel you trust and turn to for advice. Other important characteristics include humility, the ability to listen, and an insatiable curiosity. Don't limit yourself to people just like yourself. Welcome diversity! Seek someone from a different ethnic group or of the opposite gender. (If you do select someone of the opposite sex, keep the relationship strictly professional.)

The courtship ritual for attracting a mentor is similar to the ritual of dating. Introduce yourself and if you seem to "click" with the person, invite him or her for coffee or a bite to eat, and the relationship flourishes or flounders from there. (If the relationship flounders after the initial get-together, don't blame yourself. Just because you're looking for a mentor doesn't mean that the person you've selected is interested in taking on the job.)

When the relationship flourishes, the person may invite you to attend a special program at his or her business association and then may ask to see some of the projects you're doing for work. He or she will make suggestions, offer advice, and provide moral support. You'll keep him or her posted by phone or e-mail on how you're doing, and you'll get together for lunch once a month where you'll exchange views about the business. Before you know it, your business friendship has evolved into a mentor-protégé relationship, and you are both richer for it.

To make the most of that relationship, keep these guidelines in mind:

◾ *Understand your strengths and weaknesses.* This will help you and your mentor to create action plans that address areas of need.

◾ *Share your goals.* Your mentor can't help you achieve them if he or she doesn't know what they are.

■ *Set an agenda.* Decide how much time you and your mentor will spend together and agree about what you will accomplish during those times.

■ *Keep in contact.* Between the times you and your mentor get together, stay in touch through phone calls and e-mail. Tell your mentor about your progress and ask for help when you feel you're not making progress.

BECOMING A MENTOR

As you are enriched by being a protégé, you have the chance to enrich others by becoming a mentor. Don't think you have to be in your career for years before you share with others the knowledge you've gained. Even after only a year in your profession, you have a wealth of information to share with those coming up behind you.

Look for a protégé who feels as strongly about his or her goals as you feel about yours, someone who is as committed as you to making success a reality. Make it easy for the business friendship to begin. Reach out with an invitation to an after-work get together. By spending even an hour with a person, you'll be able to tell if you can make the person's career path a little less rocky.

As a mentor, you'll share suggestions, offer advice, provide guidance. To make the most of that relationship, keep these guidelines in mind:

■ *Allow your protégé to find his or her own road.* Your job is to point the person in the right direction.

■ *Find out how your protégé learns.* Some people learn by being shown examples, others need to discuss various approaches, still others have to try things themselves to find out what works. When you figure out how your protégé learns, you can help him or her best by adopting that method of teaching.

■ *Focus on strengths to improve weaknesses.* You'll want to help your protégé improve areas of weakness. To do that, focus on their areas of strength and show how those strengths can be used to improve weak areas.

■ *Watch what you say.* Your words can confuse or wound your protégé even when they're meant to encourage the person. Think before you speak and reflect on how you would feel hearing your words spoken by your mentor.

You'll get a kick out of seeing your protégé progress just as your mentor enjoyed watching your advancement. You may also be amazed at one of the secrets of being a mentor—you often learn more than the person you're coaching.

HOW LIFE-LONG LEARNING CONTRIBUTES TO LIFE-LONG SUCCESS

According to President John F. Kennedy, "Leadership and learning are indispensable to each other." If you're under the impression that graduation means an end to all learning, you're mistaken. Successful people are life-long learners. They know that learning empowers them and provides the means to move forward in pursuit of their careers and professional goals.

Unless you've chosen a career in which continuing education is mandatory, such as for keeping a license or attaining certain status in your field, continuing education will be your responsibility. If so, make a life goal right now to stay current in your industry.

Think of it this way. Businesses understand the need to enhance existing products. They tinker and tweak so that the product is more valuable and current with the latest technology.

You are your own product, and you need to be the latest and the hottest one on the market. You need to know your field, where it's going, and how to keep up with it. Unless you keep learning—enhancing the existing product—people coming up behind you will have more current knowledge of your industry than you do, and you'll be left in the dust. You'll be an obsolete product that nobody will want.

If you haven't already done so, go back to Chapter One and the *My Goals* exercise and add life-long learning to your list of long-term goals. Later in this chapter, you'll make objectives for accomplishing that goal, then follow up by adding something to your daily list of things to do tomorrow that will help you start reaching your objectives right away.

WAYS TO BECOME A LIFE-LONG LEARNER

You can become a life-long learner in a number of low-tech to high-tech ways, but the basic idea is to never stop learning. As a bonus, you'll also find that learning is much more fun when your purpose is to better yourself rather than just to be ready for a pop quiz. Here are some ways you can begin your life-long learning.

1. *Read magazines and professional journals.* Whether delivered to your home or to your office at work, magazines and professional journals bring up-to-date information to you monthly or weekly. Almost every industry has at least one trade magazine. Choose one or two that are most relevant to your career and subscribe. Because periodicals are part of your professional development, you will probably be able to get your company to spring for the subscription costs. Once the issues start arriving, plan time in your schedule to read the features and columns.

Make the most of your reading time. First, scan the table of contents to see what's being offered in a particular issue then choose to read only the articles that interest you. Be selective. Don't think you have to read every journal from cover to cover.

Next, prioritize the articles you need to read. On the table of contents page, rank the articles you need to read in #1, #2, #3, etc., order with #1 representing the article of highest interest that you will read first. Prioritize the articles you need to read so that your reading supports specific areas of interest or current work projects.

Before reading an article, glance at the subheads within the piece which serve as an outline to the article. Scanning the subheads allows you to see the focus of the article to decide if it's really of interest. If an article lacks subheads, glance quickly through the text of the piece. That is often enough to help you decide if this is a feature you'll want to read in full.

After reading an article, put a checkmark next to the title in the table of contents. This shows that you've read a particular article and prevents you from starting the piece only to realize partially through that you've already read it. This is particularly helpful if you read a journal over a two or three-week period of time.

Use a ball-point pen or highlighter to note any items of interest for follow-up. Then on the cover of the magazine write the page number of the marked item. After you finish reading the issue, the page numbers will lead you back to those items you noted. Clip and file articles that you think will be helpful to you.

Also clip the articles you don't have time to read. Put them in a folder which you carry in your briefcase at all times so you can read while you're waiting. When you're having your car serviced or when you're left to cool your heels while waiting for a client, you can plow through an article or two. You could catch up with your reading while at the doctor's or dentist's office or during your lunch hour.

Articles you read in magazine and professional journals provide a great way to start conversations with others when networking. You can ask if the person has heard about the latest advance in an area. If the person hasn't heard about it, you can offer to send a copy of the article. People start paying attention to you when you know something before they do.

As you grow in your career, eliminate subscriptions to magazines you no longer enjoy or that no longer meet your continuing education needs. Put the funds toward magazines and journals that match your current level of professional growth.

2. *Read books.* In addition to magazines and professional journals, read the latest books on career success, motivation, and in areas of specific interest to you. Each chapter in this book includes a section called *Read All About It* which provides suggestions to further your knowledge in given areas. Use those lists as starting points.

Before purchasing a book, scan the jacket copy to decide if the book is appropriate for your needs. Then read the table of contents to get an overview of the book's scope. You may be able to read only those chapters of special interest.

Plan your reading even if you're able to manage only one chapter a week. Read with a packet of index cards and a pen next to you, so you can take notes on your reading. For example, the concepts in Stephen Covey's book *First Things First* may be so meaningful to you that you capture his philosophy on the index cards and refer back to them during the week.

You can also use the index cards to refresh your memory before reading a new chapter. This helps you to get up to speed with the book before plunging into another chapter. In this way, you have continuity in your reading even though you may read each book in a piecemeal fashion.

3. *Listen to educational and motivational audiotapes.* Wouldn't it be great to have master sales trainer Tom Hopkins or motivational speaker Anthony Robbins sitting right next to you in your car as you drive to work? While these experts can't physically be in your car, their pearls of wisdom can echo from your cassette tape player.

    Most bookstores and libraries feature educational and motivational audiotapes. They're excellent ways to keep your mind active with new thoughts and ideas, using time that would otherwise be wasted while you're stuck in gridlock.

4. *Participate in Internet news and chat groups.* Expand your networking capabilities worldwide by participating in Internet news and chat groups. Find these groups through USENET or LISTSERV directories available at your public library. When you become aware of and join a new group, monitor the postings for several days to determine if the group will meet your needs.

    Participating in Internet groups has its own set of etiquette rules which you can usually find in a Frequently-Asked-Questions (FAQ) file that you can download. Obey the rules, or you risk getting flamed or even worse—having your e-mail box stuffed with thousands of unwanted messages. Present yourself as a professional at all times, offer assistance to those who post questions, and be an active participant asking your own questions and posing discussion topics.

    With some active groups, you may encounter a newsgroup directory logging hundreds of messages a day. Many of these postings may discuss conversation threads that hold little interest for you. Scan the sub-ject headings and decide which ones to read and which ones to skip. Some Internet service providers offer a filtering device that sorts e-mail into separate category mail boxes. You can set up numerous category mail boxes and let the system do the sorting for you.

5. *Attend seminars.* Seminars are information-packed educational events. They can run for an hour, a half-day, or a full day. Not only do they provide the latest developments in your field, they also serve as great events at which to sharpen your networking skills.

Find seminar announcements in magazines or professional journals, in your company's library or resource center, or through your professional associations. Once you attend a seminar, your name is added to the mailing list and other offerings are sent to you.

A typical seminar asks you to register in advance, and you receive an admission card to bring with you to the seminar site. There you'll receive an agenda and learning materials for the day. Before most seminars kick off, you have a chance to grab a beverage then meet and greet other seminar participants. Bring plenty of business cards.

The seminar may offer a single information session or several break-out sessions from which to choose. If several sessions are offered during the same time period, most seminars make audiocassette tapes of all the sessions available for later purchase. If you're torn between two great sessions offered at the same time, you can attend the one that holds the most interest for you then buy a cassette of the other one.

An all-day seminar usually features lunch on your own, so during the morning sessions scope out someone you might enjoy going to lunch with. This is an excellent chance to do more one-on-one networking, and you might even become fast friends with your lunch buddy.

Most seminars offer certificates of completion at the end of the day, and some seminars even qualify for continuing education units (CEUs). If CEUs are applicable in your profession, ask someone staffing the registration table about qualifying for them.

6. *Take continuing education courses.* While seminars give you a taste of life-long learning, continuing education courses provide a literal smorgasbord. You'll find courses in business, psychology, microcomputer technology, communication, financial management, recreation, hobbies, and more.

   If there were courses at school that you wanted to take but couldn't fit into your schedule, you can probably find equivalents in the continuing education department of your local two-year or four-year college. The courses are non-credit so you don't have to worry about doing papers or preparing for finals, and the courses are also affordable.

   A continuing education course that you should definitely consider is one in financial management or financial planning. Once you start earning money, you'll need to know how to manage your funds, set up a workable budget, and make sure you have money tucked away for retirement. Sure, retirement is years away, but experts will tell you that it's never too early to start planning.

   If getting to a classroom course at night doesn't fit into your current schedule, don't worry. Many colleges now offer on-line courses that you can take at any time.

   Check with the school's continuing education department for schedule information and ask to be put on their mailing list. That way you'll have a built-in system for reminding you at least once a semester that learning is an on-going process and that you need to be an active participant.

Use the following exercise to plan your life-long learning goals.

MY NEVER-STOP-LEARNING GOALS

■ *PURPOSE:* To plan your life-long learning goals.

1. Review your life goals and career objective and list in the space provided the education you will need to accomplish those goals.

_____

_____

_____

_____

_____

_____

2. Review your list of educational needs and prioritize them in the space provided, assigning #1 to the educational need with the highest priority, #2 to the educational need with the next highest priority, etc.

_____

_____

_____

_____

_____

3. Create a section in your day planner labeled *Educational Goals*. Write your educational needs in this section and review it every week, so you can include in your weekly planning the steps to achieve your educational goals. Update this section as your goals change or as you realize the need for new educational goals.

BUILDING BLOCKS OF COMMITMENT TO SUCCESS

*O*nce you've determined what is important to you, you need to create building blocks of commitment to success. These building blocks are all the items you put into your daily planner that allow you to create your own successful life.

For example, you may decide that staying physically fit will help to create success in your life. Being in good shape will allow you to have more energy, stamina, and be more alert to take advantage of business opportunities. You may decide that running three miles every morning will help you to stay physically fit. Then create "morning run" as a building block of commitment into your daily schedule. Once the building block is in place, it will work as a reminder that during that time period every day you have a commitment to yourself to run three miles.

If family is important to you, create building blocks for family time. If your friends are important to you, create building blocks for socializing. If your spiritual life is important to you, create building blocks for reflection, prayer, and worship. Each building block of commitment that you create contributes to a strong wall of success that will stand the test of time.

SOARING TO SUCCESS

*S*uccess is not measured by the amount of money you have in the bank. Success is a way of life that can be measured by the amount of good feelings you have every day and throughout the years. These feelings result from the progress you make in attaining your goals and becoming the person you set out to become.

Measure your success against your own vision of a fulfilled life. Whether your dream is to work as a self-employed entrepreneur or as a top-level executive in an international firm, you can measure success not by how far away you are from your goal but by how much of your time is spent in taking steps toward becoming the person you want to be. When you reach that part on your journey of a thousand miles, you'll cease creeping along the path and you'll soar to success.

Since you've taken the time to create a road map for your journey to success, stick to the direction you've outlined for yourself to follow. Continue to use this book as a guide along the way and as a reminder of where you started out and how far you've come toward achieving your dreams and living a successful life. Good luck and enjoy the journey!

And when you start soaring, as you will, keep in mind that the sky's your only limit!

Read All About It!

Biehl, Bobb. *Mentoring: Confidence in Finding a Mentor & Becoming One*. Nashville, TN: Broadman & Holman Publishers, 1997.

Cameron, Randolph W. *The Minority Executives' Handbook: The Complete Guide to Career Success in Today's Culturally Diverse Workforce*. New York, NY: Warner Books, 1997.

Carew, Jack. *The Mentor: 15 Keys to Success in Sales, Business and Life*. New York, NY: Donald I. Fine, 1998.

Corbin, Bill, & Kim Corbin. *Getting, Keeping and Growing in Your Job: A Practical Guide to Success in the 90's Workplace*. Indianapolis, IN: Jist Works, 1997.

Dilenschneider, Robert L., & Mary Jane Genova. *The Critical 14 Years of Your Professional Life*. Secaucus, NJ: Carol Publishing Group, 1997.

Dryden, Gordon & Jeannette Vos. *The Learning Revolution: A Life-Long Learning Program for the World's Finest Computer Your Amazing Brain*. Rolling Hills Estates, CA: Jalmar Press, 1994.

Green, Gordon, W. *Getting Ahead at Work*. Secaucus, NJ: Lyle Stuart, 1989.

Haldane, Bernard, & Peter F. Drucker. *Career Satisfaction and Success: A Guide to Job and Personal Freedom.* Indianapolis, IN: Jist Works, 1995.

Hendricks, William. *Coaching, Mentoring, and Managing: Breakthrough Strategies to Solve Performance Problems.* Franklin Lakes, NY: The Career Press, 1996.

Huang, Al Chungliang, and Jerry Lynch. *Mentoring: The Tao of Giving and Receiving Wisdom.* San Francisco, CA: Harper San Francisco, 1995.

Kelley, Robert E. *How to Be a Star at Work: Nine Breakthrough Strategies You Need to Succeed.* New York, NY: Times Books, 1998.

Kiewra, Kenneth, & Nelson F. Dubois. *Learning to Learn: Making the Transition from Student to Life-Long Learner.* Needham Heights, MA: Allyn & Bacon, 1997.

Shea, Gordon F. *Mentoring: How to Develop Successful Mentor Behaviors.* Los Altos, CA: Crisp Publications, 1998.

Sinetar, Marsha. *The Mentor's Spirit: Life Lessons on Leadership and the Art of Encouragement.* New York, NY: St. Martin's Press, 1998.

Wild, Russell. *Business Briefs: 165 Guiding Principles from the World's Sharpest Minds.* Princeton, NJ: Petersons Guides, 1996.

Books I've Read

Use the space provided to list the books you've read in this subject area and to reflect on what you've learned from reading them.

1. _____
2. _____
3. _____
4. _____
5. _____

Internet Resources

http://www.onlinelearning.net   This Web site provides information about on-line courses offered by the University of California Los Angeles.

Use a search engine and the following key words to find information related to topics in this chapter: *mentors, mentoring, life-long learning, adult learning, continuing education courses, on-line courses.*

My Favorite Internet Sites

Use the space provided to list your favorite Internet sites.

1. _____

2. _____

3. _____

4. _____

5. _____

SELF-ASSESSMENT

AFTER YOU HAVE FINISHED

Now that you have finished working through Career Success: Right Here, Right Now!, check the progress you have made. Read each of the following statements. Then check "yes," or "maybe," or "no" to indicate whether the statement applies to you right now.

1. I can explain my most important values and beliefs to another person.

    ❑ Yes   ❑ Maybe   ❑ No

2. I have a dream for my future.

    ❑ Yes   ❑ Maybe   ❑ No

3. I have action plans for achieving my goals.

    ❑ Yes   ❑ Maybe   ❑ No

4. I can match my skills and interests to one or more suitable occupations by using career resources.

    ❑ Yes   ❑ Maybe   ❑ No

5. I have a good resumé and can write a good cover letter.

    ❑ Yes   ❑ Maybe   ❑ No

6. I am good at preparing for and undergoing job interviews.

    ❑ Yes   ❑ Maybe   ❑ No

7. I am good at understanding the needs of other people.

    ❑ Yes   ❑ Maybe   ❑ No

8. I am an active listener who respects the speaker and understands the speaker's message.

❏ Yes ❏ Maybe ❏ No

9. I am a good speaker, with good voice qualities and good command of standard English.

❏ Yes ❏ Maybe ❏ No

10. I use a planner and a "to do" list to organize my time.

❏ Yes ❏ Maybe ❏ No

11. I can evaluate whether a job fits into my long-term professional goals.

❏ Yes ❏ Maybe ❏ No

12. I enjoy learning new things.

❏ Yes ❏ Maybe ❏ No

Review your self-assessment. Check the statements to which you answered "maybe" or "no." These statements show areas of potential growth for you.

Compare this self-assessment to the one you did when you started this book. Which areas reflect changes from "maybe" or "no" to "yes?" Great! You've made progress! Which areas are still marked "maybe" or "no?" Those are the special areas you have to put more effort into.

Reread the sections of this book that pertain to those areas, paying attention to some of the additional book and Internet resources that can help you. Then create action plans for those areas that need some more attention.

Success is a process of small steps in the direction of your dreams. You can do it—one step at a time, one foot in front of the other. *Good luck!*

SUCCESS: Interview Notes

To help you achieve both interview and career success, the following Interview Notes have been included to use as you continue your journey toward a rewarding career path. These pages allow you to track your job search progression from *when* an initial resumé was sent to *when* you obtain an interview to *when* that job offer may be made. These journal pages also allow you to honestly critique your impressions of the interview in writing. Refer to Chapter Three—Success Before, During, and After the Interview for further comments and suggestions on how to become a successful interviewer.

After each interview, go back and review your notes to see where you have improved. What were the results? Did you learn something new? What could you have done differently? Did the interview help you decide if you were the right person for the job? Keep these notes handy and review them often. In case your first job does not become a lifelong position, these notes will serve as a great tool for review in preparation for future interviews. They are yet one more step on your road to career success, right here, right now!

Interview No. 1

Date resumé sent: _____

Date of interview: _____ Interview time: _____

Company name: _____

Company address: _____

_____

_____

Telephone number: _____

FAX number: _____

Contact person(s):   e-mail address: _____

1. _____

2. _____

3. _____

4. _____

5. _____

Interview Comments:

What went well? _____

_____

_____

_____

What could be improved?

_____

_____

_____

_____

Interview Follow-up:

_____

Date thank you letter sent:

_____

_____

Date of follow-up phone call:

_____

_____

Second interview date:

_____

_____

Third interview date:

_____

_____

Job offer date:

_____

_____

Acceptance of job offer date:

_____

_____

Start date:

_____

_____

Interview No. 2

Date resumé sent: _____

Date of interview: _____ Interview time: _____

Company name: _____

Company address: _____

_____

_____

Telephone number: _____

FAX number: _____

Contact person(s): _____ e-mail address: _____

1. _____

2. _____

3. _____

4. _____

5. _____

Interview Comments:

What went well? _____

_____

_____

_____

What could be improved?

_____

_____

_____

_____

_____

Interview Follow-up:

Date thank you letter sent:

_____

_____

Date of follow-up phone call:

_____

_____

Second interview date:

_____

_____

Third interview date:

_____

_____

Job offer date:

_____

_____

Acceptance of job offer date:

_____

_____

Start date:

_____

_____

Interview No. 3

Date resumé sent:

Date of interview: Interview time:

Company name:

Company address:

Telephone number:

FAX number:

Contact person(s):   e-mail address:

1.

2.

3.

4.

5.

Interview Comments:

What went well?

What could be improved?

_____

_____

_____

_____

Interview Follow-up:

Date thank you letter sent:

_____

_____

Date of follow-up phone call:

_____

_____

Second interview date:

_____

_____

Third interview date:

_____

_____

Job offer date:

_____

_____

Acceptance of job offer date:

_____

_____

Start date:

_____

_____

Interview No. 4

Date resumé sent:

Date of interview: Interview time:

Company name:

Company address:

Telephone number:

FAX number:

Contact person(s):   e-mail address:

1.

2.

3.

4.

5.

Interview Comments:

What went well?

What could be improved?

Interview Follow-up:

Date thank you letter sent:

Date of follow-up phone call:

Second interview date:

Third interview date:

Job offer date:

Acceptance of job offer date:

Start date:

Interview No. 5

Date resumé sent:

Date of interview: _____ Interview time:

Company name:

Company address:

Telephone number:

FAX number:

Contact person(s): _____ e-mail address:

1.

2.

3.

4.

5.

Interview Comments:

What went well?

Interview Comments (continued):

What could be improved?

_____

_____

_____

_____

Interview Follow-up:

_____

Date thank you letter sent:

_____

_____

Date of follow-up phone call:

_____

_____

Second interview date:

_____

_____

Third interview date:

_____

_____

Job offer date:

_____

_____

Acceptance of job offer date:

_____

_____

Start date:

_____

_____

Interview No. 6

Date resumé sent:

Date of interview: Interview time:

Company name:

Company address:

Telephone number:

FAX number:

Contact person(s):   e-mail address:

1.

2.

3.

4.

5.

Interview Comments:

What went well?

Interview Comments (continued):

What could be improved?

_____

_____

_____

_____

Interview Follow-up:

Date thank you letter sent:

_____

Date of follow-up phone call:

_____

Second interview date:

_____

Third interview date:

_____

Job offer date:

_____

Acceptance of job offer date:

_____

Start date:

_____

Interview No. 7

Date resumé sent:

Date of interview: Interview time:

Company name:

Company address:

Telephone number:

FAX number:

Contact person(s):   e-mail address:

1.

2.

3.

4.

5.

Interview Comments:

What went well?

Interview Comments (continued):

What could be improved?

_____

_____

_____

_____

Interview Follow-up:

Date thank you letter sent:

_____

Date of follow-up phone call:

_____

Second interview date:

_____

Third interview date:

_____

Job offer date:

_____

Acceptance of job offer date:

_____

Start date:

_____

_____

Interview No. 8

Date resumé sent:

Date of interview: Interview time:

Company name:

Company address:

Telephone number:

FAX number:

Contact person(s):   e-mail address:

1.

2.

3.

4.

5.

Interview Comments:

What went well?